FINDING HEAVEN

FINDING HEAVEN

STORIES OF GOING HOME

———

Christopher de Vinck

LOYOLAPRESS.

CHICAGO

LOYOLAPRESS.
3441 N. ASHLAND AVENUE
CHICAGO, ILLINOIS 60657
(800) 621-1008
WWW.LOYOLABOOKS.ORG

Interior and cover design by Eileen Wagner

Library of Congress Cataloging-in-Publication Data

De Vinck, Christopher, 1951–
    Finding heaven : stories of going home / Christopher de Vinck
        p. cm.
    ISBN 0-8294-1646-3
        1. Heaven—Christianity. I. Title.

BT846.3 .D4 2002
236'.24—dc21

2001050234

Printed in the United States

Contents

I never saw a moor,
I never saw the sea;
Yet know I how the heather looks,
And what a wave must be.

I never spoke with God,
Nor visited in heaven;
Yet certain am I of the spot
As if the chart were given.

Emily Dickinson

A Message from Australia

One evening, as I was adjusting my son's blanket before kissing him good night, he looked up at me and asked, "Dad, do we know anyone who is old and who lives in Australia?" I stopped pulling up the blanket, looked at Michael, and asked, "Why?"

"Well, when he dies, he can contact us with a message that there is a heaven. If I knew for sure that there was a heaven, it would make all the difference in the world."

What does Australia have to do with a profession of faith in the mind of a ten-year-old boy? Well, if you live in New Jersey, Australia is far away, much closer to paradise than, say, Trenton. In the mind of a child, if you die in Australia, you are already well on your way to heaven.

I smiled again as I sat down on the side of Michael's bed and asked, "Do you know that your grandmother loves you very much?"

"Yes," Michael answered.

"And you can't see her right now, but you know she is there. Heaven is like that."

"But I can call Grammy on the phone. There aren't any telephones in heaven."

Michael wanted definitive proof of heaven—a videotape, a telegram, even a signed picture would do: *Dear Michael, Best Wishes, God.*

It is Easter Sunday as I write, 6:28 in the morning. Today is the holy of holy days in the Christian calendar, the day we believe that life begins. It is a day for us to make a public declaration that heaven exists. It is the day that we publicly celebrate that there are telephone lines to heaven. We lay aside the palms, forgo the Lenten sacrifices, light candles and sing to God, "You are the light of the world." Faith is knowing for sure that your grandmother loves you, even though you cannot see her.

My son had said something profound, "*If I knew for sure that there was a heaven, it would make all the difference in the world.*"

Yes! Exactly! Know the existence of heaven, and our daily struggles become marked with the dance. Know the existence of heaven, and the candle conquers all darkness. Know the existence of heaven, and we live a life built upon mercy, compassion, hope. We live with a destiny that can be explained to a ten-year-old child and to an old dying man in Australia: "We are on our way home to the Lord." To know that each step we take is one more step toward heaven gives us joy in our routines, acceptance in our losses, companionship in our loneliness. Yes, to know for sure that there is a heaven does make all the difference in the world.

Michael knew this when he was ten years old.

I sensed it too when I was his age. One day, when I was ten years old, I said to myself with confidence, "I am going to find heaven." I thought I knew how.

I had a cat called Bissy, a black cat, long and sleek, with gold eyes and a pink tongue. Each evening, I would stand on the back porch, cup my hands over my mouth, and call out in a loud voice, "Bissy! Here, Bissy! Bissy! Bissy! Bissy! Bissy!" From deep within the woods that darkened the back end of my parents' property, I would hear a stirring of leaves. I would call out again, "Bissy!" and a black spot would emerge at the lip of the woods. With another call, Bissy would run up the back lawn, leap over the low rock wall, and zoom past the bird feeder and up the porch stairs, where she would jump into my arms.

Then I would carry my cat to my bed, where she slept at my feet every night since I was five years old.

But one evening, after a late supper, I stood on the porch and called for my cat. Silence. I called again. The trees stood firm and tall. I called again. No cat.

For three weeks I stepped outside and called out, "Bissy! Bissy! Bissy!" At the beginning of the fourth week, my mother said to me that Bissy went to heaven. She assured me that when I die someday and go to heaven, Bissy will run up to me and leap into my arms again, and I believed her. Because Bissy simply disappeared, because I never buried her or found her dead body, I assumed that she "went to heaven," as my mother said. Bissy *went* to heaven like my father *went* to work. My grandparents *went* back to Belgium at the end of each summer. We *went* to church on Sundays. *Went* means there is a starting point and a destination. But I didn't want to wait to see my cat again; I decided to find heaven and bring my cat home.

I made no particular preparation for my journey. I was no Jacques Cousteau, or Darwin, or Columbus. All I knew was that my cat had entered the woods and had never returned, so I believed that she had discovered a way to heaven there, perhaps behind a rock or deep inside a holly bush. I would find the way. I had no equipment, though I did break off a stick from the mock orange bush and used it as my sword. Whenever I entered the woods, I always carried a good stick because I liked to chop at the skunk cabbage that draped itself along the way like giant, green elephant ears.

I followed a path that split my father's woods in half. The path wove down a slope, past a large rock to the right, and over a small stone bridge my father had built, which crossed a trickling stream. Bissy and I had walked along this path hundreds of times. It seemed to me that if the path to heaven were along the regular route, she and I would have surely found it long ago. So after I crossed the little bridge, I left the path. I stepped to my left and into the thick bushes, where I immediately startled a woodcock. It startled *me* when it flew out of its hiding place and beyond my reach and vision, quickly disappearing between branches and thick spring leaves.

I was more delighted than frightened. I threw my arms above my head and waved my stick. I thought it was a great day when a boy finds a woodcock in his father's woods. In fact, I have never seen a woodcock anywhere else.

Since I had discovered *something*, I continued walking to the left, toward the barbed-wire fence at the outer edge of my father's property. I found honeysuckle cascading over the fence. The trumpet flowers hung down from their green stems and breathed a fragrance that gave me a sense that they had magical powers. My sister Anne and I believed honeysuckle was magic. We would make honeysuckle crowns for our heads and she played the queen and I her king.

Perhaps the entrance to heaven was on the fence—out along the seams of the universe somehow held together with a thread of honeysuckle. I crawled behind the draping honeysuckle vine and did not find Bissy. I did not find the portal to heaven there.

All afternoon I looked for my cat. I followed rabbit footprints in the mud thinking perhaps they would lead me to a place where I had never been: a hutch, or hole, a hidden warren tended by Farmer McGregor . . . perhaps, surely one of God's apostles. (When I was a child I identified many people as God's apostles, for I had confused what I learned in church about apostles and thought they were really God in disguise, something like Santa Claus or old Josh, my neighbor's grandfather who spoke only Polish, looked like an ancient wood carving, liked my sister and me, and grew fat peppers in his garden that was ringed with aluminum pie plates to frighten away the crows and grackles.)

I did not find heaven *that* afternoon. I did come across the biggest jack-in-the-pulpit I had ever seen: three smooth leaves, a striped green-and-deep-purple flower in the shape of a monk's hood, and under the hood the small, hidden "Jack," a mass of tiny flowers shaped like a little club. I bent over, lifted the hood of the jack-in-the-pulpit, closed one eye, and looked deep inside. No keyhole to heaven.

I walked out of the woods in the late afternoon and found my father burning winter detritus: dried leaves and sticks he raked up from the lawn and driveway. I spent the rest of the late afternoon poking my mock orange stick into the flames as the smoke encircled my father and me.

No, I did not find the path to heaven *that* day, but I did find during my journey into the woods a sense for it all. The woods were filled with little gods of happiness hidden in the trumpets of the honeysuckle and under the hood of the jack-in-the-pulpit. Perhaps the rabbits turn into gnomes and carry cats away to heaven. These are the things I believed when I was ten.

Today I believe in the existence of heaven whenever I smell the honeysuckle. Heaven is a place for the pure of heart, and I know that children have a purity of heart, and I remember what it was like to be a child. I believe that we can find evidence of God's existence if we look back to our lives and take notice of the patterns: Oh, *that* is why I lost that job; it led me to this other job. Oh, *that* is why I went to that party; it is how I met my husband. Our lives are not like metal balls being flung through a pinball machine, arbitrarily bouncing from one point to the next. No, I believe we move along in a purposeful journey with choices placed before us.

We can find the path to heaven by taking a backward glance to our lives with knowledge and see God's influence upon us. We can find the existence of God in the present moment as the sun rises this Easter morning. And we can look to the future with faith based on what we already know. We walk in faith, but conviction of God's love comes to us through the combination of faith and knowledge, not on faith alone.

Last weekend my son Michael and I walked through my father's woods, the same woods I explored as a child. Michael is now seventeen. He stepped off the path to the left and startled a woodcock; he raised his arms in glee; he saw with the eyes of a child. He is building confidence in his own pure heart. These memories of goodness will sustain him during his days of adult doubt. We must battle against doubt all of our lives, and the more clearly we can look back and see God's will, the more courage we will have to maintain faith in God's existence.

There's a pattern to God's work. Salvation is found in the backward glance at original love. We see cycles. Nature replicates itself each year. We seem to be moving forward, but the seasons moving forward are, in actuality, just repeating the message of creation over and over again, and in the message of creation is the promise of rebirth. We did not "come into the world"; we were born *of* the world, uprooted from the soil and conferred with a dignity of an inexplicable intention. We live a life of implicit reasons. Perhaps God is a poet, speaking to us in the language of metaphors: spring—the hope of heaven; sun—the cycle of my coming to you each day; sleep—the time of passage to a distant place called peace.

We can find our way to God and to his heaven in looking at these patterns. We get a glimpse of God's doing in the memories of our lives, and in the present moment of those we love, and in pursuit of the vocations we stumbled upon.

If we pursue our lives looking for hints of heaven both in our past and in our present moment, we will be able to take a backward glance and see, exactly see, the evidence that we are, indeed, on the path to heaven. We will know that we are not lost.

As clearly stated in Vatican II's Pastoral Constitution on the Church in the Modern World, "The future of humanity lies in the hands of those who are strong enough to provide coming generations with reasons for loving and hoping." We can detect the love of God in our own spiritual autobiographies, in the influence of those who provide us with reasons for living and loving. Here is where we loved our mothers, and oh yes, here is a teacher who wrote a kind word on our essays; this is where we felt the pain of loss; this is where we learned the joy of sharing. And yes, right here in our twenties is where we knew who we would marry.

We are surrounded by love. Love is the present condition. Learning how to love was the condition of our past. Teaching others how to love is the condition of the future.

Easter Sunday replicates the good news: Christ is risen. For more than two thousand years we have been celebrating the proof of Christ's resurrection from death. Either we believe in perpetual death or we believe in perpetual life. It makes all the difference in the world. I tell my son, "Look back to the history of the world, and you will find Christ walking among us, spreading the good news." I will tell my son always, "Look back at your own life and seek evidence of that good news playing upon your own destiny."

This little book is the best evidence I can produce to show my children that God's promise of salvation is true. It is here in these pages that I place little stones on the ground for my son to follow as he looks for a way home to God.

I

CHILDHOOD

Heaven Is Up

One of the great moments of my spiritual awakening is indelibly associated in my memory with the smell of pine-tree sap. It was the denouement of an adventure—and perhaps a miracle—that showed me the direction to heaven.

As a child I wanted to climb all the trees in the garden. The house where I grew up was surrounded by two and a half acres of lawns, trees, and woods. The woods were filled with skunk cabbage in the spring and snow tracks of rabbits in the winter. All children ought to have at least two acres of wilderness for exploration and spiritual development. Christopher Robin had his Hundred Acre Woods. Christopher de Vinck had his two and a half, and that was just right.

If I could climb to the top of every tree on our property, I reasoned, I would be king. There would be nothing higher than me. This was a childish hint of adult obsessions with power and might. We are obsessed with being the best: building the tallest building, owning the most property, having the highest salary, owning the fastest car, attending the most prestigious university. I knew as a child that power had something to do with being at the top, so I decided to climb to the top of every tree in the yard and claim victory over the wild land that was my father's property.

The maple tree was the easiest to climb, for it grew thick, wide branches that extended like gnarled fingers and formed a natural ladder for me to climb. The oak tree was difficult at first, for there were no low branches. I had to nail thin slats of wood into the trunk to make my own rungs to reach the branches. From the top of an old oak, I strained my eyes to see the Empire State Building. We lived thirty miles from New York City, and we could see the city skyline from the hill on Crescent Avenue, north of town.

The hardest tree to climb was the pine tree on the front lawn. It was difficult for two reasons: the branches were numerous and close together, and the last quarter of the tree's top was thin and thus prone to swaying. The tree stood three stories tall. I stood at its base and imagined that I was Jack from *Jack and the Beanstalk*. If Jack could make it, I thought, so could I. I grabbed the first, low branch and pulled myself up into the tree, hugging the trunk along the way.

The higher I climbed, the more difficult my task became. I found myself battling the branches that protruded from the trunk: the long, thick branches that pointed straight down; the thin, little branches that shot straight out; and the dead branches that liked to stick into the sides of invading little boys.

I had seven or eight more feet to go when I began to rock back and forth. At the top, the trunk was no wider than the thinnest branch. I grabbed it and hung on. I wrapped my legs around the top of the tree, but the more I tried to steady myself, the more the tree swayed. It was as if I was at the top of a metronome, ticking back and forth, back and forth. I felt as if I was holding onto the tip of a dragon's tail and it was trying to flick me off. I looked down at my house, where my family was preparing the dining room table for Mass. I looked down at the car in the driveway and at the empty lawn chairs that sat on the grass like content, grazing cows. I thought I was going to die.

And then I let go.

I have since read of people falling from four-story buildings and walking away, miraculously uninjured. I have seen news coverage of people who have survived plane crashes and train wrecks. I didn't know of these things when

I was seven, tumbling down, down, down the side of the pine tree. But my fall would be just as miraculous. It was as if the branches extended like arms to cradle my fall. I think, even to this day, that the pine tree in front of my parents' house, the tree that cradled me, is a female tree. I bounced from branch to branch like a pinball in a pinball machine until I landed on my stomach in the driveway.

"Christopher!" my grandmother called from the front porch. "Christopher! Time for Mass!"

I stood up, brushed the dirt off my pants, and ran home. My family was already at their seats around the dining-room table, which was draped with a white cloth. I took my seat beside my grandfather, who looked down at me with a curious grin. Then my godfather, Father Raya, began the opening prayer. I wanted to lean over to my grandfather and tell him, "I almost died." But instead I said, "I climbed to the top of all the trees in the yard." He just looked down at me and smiled.

I looked down at my hands; they were covered with pine-tree sap. I showed my grandfather, and he wrinkled his nose in disapproval. My grandmother whispered that I should have washed my hands before Mass. At communion, as the taste of bread and wine mingled with the smell of sap, I knew that I could conquer anything. Now, as an adult, I still believe that with the Eucharist, with faith, and with the sap of life spread upon my hands, I can conquer everything, even death.

A few days ago, when my wife, Roe, was sitting on the couch reading, I told her that I was writing a book about my own path to heaven. She asked, "How do you know that you are going to heaven?" She smiled and then returned to the book she was reading. I was taken aback by the simplicity of the question. She was trying to tease me, but

Christmas Gift from Belgium

In a cartoon a friend once showed me, two bishops who have died together in a car accident suddenly find themselves walking arm in arm in heaven. One bishop turns to the other in amazement and says, "My God! It's all true!"

Life teaches us to avoid extravagant expectations. We have faith, but sometimes it's more like half faith and half doubt. We don't want to be disappointed. Even people who profess 100 percent certitude about things like heaven tend to admit a bit of doubt: "Well, it probably won't happen that way, but it sure would be nice."

My first serious lesson in disappointment occurred when I was ten. It was October, and my grandmother and grandfather were about to leave us and return to their home in Belgium. We would not see them again until the following summer.

"I have been thinking about Christmas," my grandmother announced as I stood in the kitchen and watched her adjust her coat and hat in preparation for the trip. Her comment instantly struck my imagination: gifts and Santa Claus. Much of my image of paradise still contains all that Christmas was for me as a boy.

"I have been talking to your grandfather, and we have come up with a wonderful Christmas idea," she continued. My grandfather reached into his coat pocket and pulled out a yellow pencil. He was a tall, dignified man with white hair. He had been a general in the Belgian army, and when he smiled, all the wrinkles in his face deepened. He ordered me to take off my shoe.

I thought about the hole in my sock and looked up at my grandfather's face. He smiled. My grandmother smiled.

I slipped off my right shoe as my grandfather pulled a piece of white typing paper out of one of the kitchen cabinets. He placed the paper on the floor and said, "Put your foot here on the paper." As my grandmother hovered over me, observing the action, my grandfather brought the pencil down and traced the outline of my foot. It tickled.

"Stand still," my grandmother kindly warned. "We want to get an exact measure."

I wiggled my toes a bit, and then the work was done. My grandfather told me to step off the paper, and when I did he picked it up and handed it to my grandmother.

"Very good," she said as she carefully folded the paper and stuffed it into her bulging purse.

I helped my father carry their suitcases to the car. My sisters, brothers, and I gathered at the front door to kiss my grandparents good-bye, and then they were gone.

During the following weeks, I tried to imagine what my grandparents would send me for Christmas. Would it be ski boots? flippers for swimming? I would have been satisfied with a pair of wool Christmas socks like the pair my grandmother made for my sister the year before, the ones with reindeer knit around the ankles, but what I really wanted was a pair of ice skates.

In December, a delivery truck pulled onto the crunchy gray stones that made up our driveway. The doorbell rang and there stood the UPS man in a brown uniform with a large box from Belgium. The Belgian Christmas gifts had arrived. I was sure mine was a pair of skates. Each winter, my sister Anne and I would skate on the frozen swamp out back and pretend we were Olympic skaters. My skates were hand-me-downs that were ripped at the toes. I hoped that the measurements my grandfather had taken were correct. I also worried that perhaps my foot had grown in the two months since he had taken the measurements and the skates would not fit.

On Christmas Eve, my mother placed all the gifts under the tree, including the ones from my grandparents, wrapped in my grandmother's typical odd-colored tissue paper and tied with curled ribbons. My father hung the stockings on the mantle of the fireplace. We said prayers at the manger of Bethlehem that my parents constructed each December on the living-room table. My sister Anne sang "O Come, O Come, Emanuel," and then my father said it was time for bed.

The next morning, Christmas morning, we five children stood at the top of the stairs and waited for my mother and father to step out of their room. When they emerged, my father called out, "One. Two. Three." And on three, we were allowed to rush down the stairs. I stopped at the Japanese prints my father had hung on the walls of the stairwell. Each Christmas, I would look into the glass over the prints and see the reflection of the Christmas tree and the lights.

"Merry Christmas! Merry Christmas!" my youngest sister called out. She sat before the tree and looked up at my mother. "Can we open the presents?" My mother nodded. That year I received Sterling North's book *Rascal,* a board game, a chocolate Santa Claus, a balsa plane with a red propeller, and a compass. At last my mother leaned over and handed me the present wrapped in my grandmother's odd-colored tissue paper. "This is from your grandparents," she said with a smile.

I took the box and set it on the living-room carpet. Off came the curled ribbon, the tissue paper, and the lid of the box. Inside was more tissue paper, which I spread open like angel wings. And there, in the center of the box, in the center of the living room, in the center of Christmas, was the ugliest pair of shoes I had ever seen.

For some reason, my grandparents had decided that the perfect Christmas gift for me would be a pair of pointed, lace-up, brown alligator-skin dress shoes. I wore, at the time, my favorite Keds sneakers.

"Shoes?" I said, looking up at my mother. "Shoes?"

"They are made from real alligator skin," my mother said. Normally I would have been impressed with alligator skin, but not on shoes.

"Wanna play Chutes and Ladders?" my sister asked. I tossed the shoes back into the box, slapped my sister on the back, called out, "Gotcha last," and the two of us ran out of the room.

The following Christmas, my grandparents sent me a cuckoo clock. At the toll of each hour, a small bird popped out from behind a little round door. When I think back on those gifts, I realize that it wasn't the gift that mattered, but my grandparents' love. I had great expectations, and in the end they were not fulfilled. But the disappointment paled in the face of love. Heaven is like that. We have expectations of what it will be like, but in the end, what it's like doesn't matter. God's love matters. That is the gift.

Einstein, Queen Elizabeth, and Sister Lillian

When someone told me as a child that there was a possibility of sitting at the right hand of God, I panicked. I heard talk of saints and angels sitting at the right hand of God. There was talk of Mary and Jesus and the Holy Ghost (the ghost part captured my interest the most), and each time I felt a twinge of fear. I knew the dangers of sitting beside my grandfather at the dinner table. My shirt wasn't tucked in enough; my hair wasn't combed right; my hands were too dirty to handle the bread basket. What must it be like to sit beside the creator of the universe?

During our honeymoon in London, Roe and I visited Madame Tussaud's famous wax museum. We walked among kings and scientists, presidents and thieves. I felt an odd sensation standing beside Einstein. It felt as if I was encroaching on his space, as if there really was a person standing beside me and not just wax, hair, and clothes. It made me uncomfortable. I strangely wondered if Einstein was uncomfortable too.

Proximity works better when combined with some distance. People don't have to be nearby to change our surroundings. Note the distinct difference between being in the house when everyone is home, and when everyone is not. The house feels different when I am alone. But it feels different if someone is there. I might not see Roe all day, but if I know she is in the house, I'm aware of some invisible connection between us, a presence, a song of the family being sung.

Our spiritual selves crave this sense of closeness to God, who often seems to absent himself from our homes. Just like my son Michael, I thought once that I could send a message to God, but mine was on the tail of kite. When I was a boy, the story about Benjamin Franklin and the key in the thunderstorm made a big impression on me. I thought he had gotten as close to God's power as I could imagine, so it made sense to send up a kite with a note to God. As an adult I have learned that some of us will try anything to communicate with God, to feel that presence beside us, to have him lean beside us so that we can feel protected.

We crave this feeling of being embraced and loved. Days can go by without anyone telling us that we are pretty, or good, or grace-filled, or precious. Our fragile selves need the embrace. Our glass-delicate selves need words of praise. The reed-self needs the wind leaning against us to define our strength.

Perhaps this is why we feel powerful in the presence of power. When my sister Anne and I were children, we traveled to Montreal with our grandparents on a tour. At a hotel for dinner one night we sat at a long, ornate table in the main dining room. At the head of the table was a large, fancy chair with crowns and birds and flowers embedded in the legs and arms. As the waiter stepped up to take our order, he leaned over to Anne and me and whispered, "The last person to sit in that chair over there was the queen of England. She was here last night for a grand dinner."

Of course Anne and I leaped from our seats and ran to the tall chair and took turns sitting right there in the queen's place. We felt grand, empowered by power.

As I grew older, I realized God was not going to sit next to me at the movie theater and that I wasn't going to send a message to God on a kite string. I was losing interest in God a little bit. God wasn't as interesting as Superman. Joey, the popular boy in my school, seemed to have more power than God. But still I wanted to feel God's presence. Just like my son Michael, who wanted a message sent back to him from heaven, I too wanted physical proof of God's existence.

Then I met Sister Lillian. Sister Lillian was a Dominican nun who wore the traditional black habit, the black veil, the stiff white collar, and the stiff white headpiece that fit along her forehead and covered her hair. Sister Lillian was beautiful. She had milk-white skin. Her voice carried a slight accent I did not recognize. Her hands were long and thin. Her wrists were covered in tight sleeves. I remember how she was able to keep handkerchiefs, pens, pencils, and hard candies somehow hidden underneath the black cloth. I liked how her long, black rosary beads dangled from her waist and sometimes clinked against my desk when she walked by during a spelling quiz. Each time Sister Lillian came near me, I felt a presence, something holy perhaps, something grand.

One fall afternoon, during recess, I stood against the school building alone, watching the other children run under the large oak tree, flip baseball cards, and jump rope. Suddenly I saw Sister Lillian emerge to my left from the main door in her flowing black-and-white habit. She nearly danced down the concrete steps, challenged a kid to a card-flipping contest, and jumped a few times under the girls' twirling gray rope. Then she saw me standing alone in the school yard. As she started to walk toward me, I was a bit frightened. I was safe at my desk as Sister Lillian wrote on the blackboard or walked down the aisles reciting a story about goats and bridges. But here, on the black-tarred parking lot, I was vulnerable.

Sister Lillian walked up to me as I stood up straight and awkward. "Christopher," Sister Lillian said without any provocation, "God loves you very much," and then she embraced me with her long arms and thin hands. I could smell her iron-pressed clothes, the chalk on her hands, and I heard her slight breath above me.

"Yes, Sister," I said, the way we were taught to speak to nuns. For some reason that very moment has always stayed with me. In fact, Sister Lillian's presence has never left me. She remains part of me—longer than the aura of the queen of England hung in that Montreal hotel. I do not know whatever became of the happy nun, but she, like an icon, was forever painted upon my wooden soul. It transformed my heart so it could happily accept God's love. Since that autumn day under the wide oak tree, the knowledge of God's love has never left me. Sister Lillian must have been a true messenger from heaven, carrying the invitation to join God at his side, because he loves me. We all have people in our lives who have pointed us toward goodness. For me the early hints of God's messengers were found in my friendship with Sister Lillian.

I haven't seen Sister Lillian since I was a boy. I do not even know if she is still alive. She doesn't know what a profound influence she had on my spiritual self. Sister Lillian did her job for me. She brought to me hints of the good news: I am worthy of love. This is the key to our spiritual selves. If God is love, then we must have a bit of God within ourselves. If God is love, we must be on our way to his kingdom. If God is love, and if I am loved, I must have come from God. If I come from God, I will return to God. We struggle all of our lives to try to make our way back home, back to a purity of heart. Sister Lillian pointed the way.

Pumpkin Boy

"If I knew for sure there was a heaven . . . " My son's statement echoes throughout my life again and again. Michael not only seeks proof of God's existence; he recognizes it as an individual search. "If I knew for sure . . . "

After all the evidence is in, after all the seeking and praying and reading and living, we have to draw our own conclusions about faith and about the reality of God's presence among us. We base these conclusions on what we know. Many people, perhaps most, come to their understanding of God's reality through simple means: the beauty of the flowers in a garden, the words of assurance from a mother, the tragic loss of a loved one, the unbidden infusion of the Holy Spirit at an unexpected moment.

Yet before we can come to this understanding, we need a solid sense of self. "If *I* knew for sure," my son said. "If I, Michael de Vinck, born on March 31, 1985, who enjoys tennis and train sets and friends and skiing, if *I* knew for sure there was a heaven, that would make all the difference in the world."

To seek God, we must also seek self. Who am I? Am I a happy person? Am I lonely? Am I a reader, swimmer, gardener, painter, singer, dancer, lover, husband, wife, sister, brother, daughter, son, baker, lawyer, butcher, writer, candlestick maker? A strong sense of self fortifies us against the inevitable challenges to our faith and identity; it fortifies us against the whims of the devil, who tries to destroy our purity of heart, and this destructive force will try and eat away at us day by day. Woe to the devil when he confronts people who know who they are: "I am a son; I am a daughter; I am a child of God. I choose love. I plant azaleas. I believe in Atticus in *To Kill a Mockingbird* and in Sydney Carton in *A Tale of Two Cities*. I am built to answer two questions in my life: who will I love, and what is my vocation?"

Periodically, the self needs healing. We have many resources to help us find this healing—our friends and family, our faith, our work, and, sometimes, professional healers. We can also do much to heal ourselves. In fact, finding the inner resources for self-healing is one of the great tasks of establishing a sound sense of self.

I learned about this years ago when I was tormented by bullies in school. I have big ears, or so I thought when I was ten. Others thought so too. I was often called Dumbo in school. For a month, I taped my ears to my head each night before going to bed, in the hopes of flattening them. I even speculated about how much it would hurt if I were to cut them off—as Vincent van Gogh had. No one in my family knew that I harbored a secret dread of my pair of auricles, which seemed to protrude from my head like radar dishes.

During this time of self-doubt, my fifth-grade teacher read aloud Washington Irving's *The Legend of Sleepy Hollow*. I loved the Galloping Hessian, the spectre who roamed on horseback through the swamps, glens, and mysterious hollows of Tarry Town. I leaned forward in my chair as my teacher read about the goblin rider tossing his pumpkin head at poor Ichabod Crane. Immediately, I decided to steal a pumpkin from the farm behind my father's woods. I had a plan and a motive. And a reason.

It was near Halloween, the time of the mask, when we are given the chance to temporarily transform ourselves into someone powerful.

I ran home under the madras skirts of the maple trees, rushed into the house, stomped up the stairs to my brother's room, and grabbed his pocketknife, which he kept hidden in a shoe box under his bed. I ran out the back door, jumped down over the five porch steps, and landed in the pile of leaves my father had raked earlier that day. I quickly checked to make sure that my brother's small knife hadn't fallen out of my pocket, and then I ran to the woods.

I felt purified when I entered the woods. I wanted to change my life. I wanted to be a strong boy with no ears.

Beyond the far end of the woods, our neighbor's October farm stretched out like a cornucopia: apples, late corn and peppers, and a field of round pumpkins lying on their sides, prepared, it seemed, to give birth. I crawled on my belly under the barbed-wire fence and crept across the field until I found a smooth, ribbed pumpkin that was the right size for my purpose. I quickly snapped the stem from the vine, stretched my arms around the waist of the pumpkin, stood up, and ran back into my father's woods.

When I was sure that no one had seen me, I sat down under a large oak tree and cut out the bottom of the pumpkin with my brother's pocketknife. I reached in through the gaping hole and scooped out the white seeds and orange goo until the pumpkin was hollow. Then I set it upright and cut out two triangle eyes, a triangle nose, and a gap-toothed smile.

Feeling like a knight about to don his suit of armor, I slowly lifted the hollow pumpkin and stuck my head through the large hole.

I was disappointed that the pumpkin didn't sit straight on my shoulders and that I had to hold it in place with my hands. I was also disappointed by the unpleasant smell. But I felt something similar to what the first Greek actors must have felt when they slipped on their theatrical masks. I was different—a new character. I was the new Galloping Hessian.

I was the new, powerful, orange-headed *earless* goblin. In my masked dance, I was the defender of the woods, my own Sleepy Hollow. "Woe to Ichabod Crane! Woe to those brats in school!"

Then my father called me in for supper. I lifted the mask off my head and dashed it against the thick trunk of the oak tree. "Take that!" I bellowed as I began to gallop home.

This was my Halloween transformation. After that evening, the taunts from the schoolboys hurt less and less, and eventually stopped. What we do in secret can often lead to a transfiguration.

The self is a battleground between God's power and the power of evil. I have remained a faith-filled person because I learned as a child how to cultivate strength and because I learned as a man how to maintain it. My mother said there was a heaven. The taunts of bullies threatened me, but I withstood them. I discovered in the woods the power of imagination. I could imagine that I was a powerful knight vanquishing my enemies. This made me better able to live as an adult according to Jesus' desire that we imagine a world where we love one another as he so loves us. God is the defender of the woods. If we dance with him, we will find our way.

Treasures in Tight Places

I believe that heaven is the home that awaits us at the end of our journey. We are all trying to make our way home, and God leads us there by placing road signs for us along the way. These road signs are our memories, personal reminders of who we are, and they point us toward God and our destiny in heaven, helping us find our way back home when we get lost. Even in a terrible childhood, there were traces of heaven, moments of joy and wonder and purity. It is these moments that we must seek out, trusting that they will lead us to God's kingdom.

In the novel *To Kill a Mockingbird,* the neighborhood recluse, Boo Radley, hides small gifts for the children, Scout and Jem, inside a rotten knothole in the trunk of an old tree. The children periodically find gum, marbles, little statues, and other small trinkets, gifts offered by the shy, slow, simple, and good Boo, who protects the children and eventually saves their lives.

We human beings like to hide things in tight places. As a child, I was fascinated by how the ancient kings of Egypt were buried with gold, food, pots, dishes, utensils. I remember how pleased I was when I discovered a small pocket hidden inside the larger pocket of my new pair of jeans. After my father explained that such was the place to keep coins, I immediately found a nickel and stuffed it deep inside the magic pouch. I remember a high-school friend who showed me the secret hiding place he had created in his wood-paneled bedroom. With the pull of a hidden string, part of a panel slid open, exposing a small chamber the size of a shoe box. Here my friend kept his money, firecrackers, a genuine Joe DiMaggio autograph, and a picture of Laura Tarpy, the prettiest girl in our freshman class.

Today I hide the key to my Model A Ford in the honey pot that sits on the shelf beside the kitchen door. My wife keeps her favorite rings and bracelets in a small velvet sack hidden deep within the items in the bottom drawer of her dresser.

Why do we do this? Of course we hide things to protect them from thieves. We stash things away in case of an emergency. An aunt of mine who lives in Belgium keeps a supply of canned food hidden behind her bookcase just in case another war breaks out in Europe. She has lived through two world wars.

We also hide things because we wish to preserve what was, to stop time, to retain something of the days that brought us joy so that we can remember them. Many people keep clothes that their babies wore or locks of their children's hair. After my grandfather died, my grandmother kept the watch he wore, and she made sure to wind it each night. She felt, in a way, that she was keeping a part of him ticking against her wrist.

I have my own secret, my own place for hidden things, and no one knows about it.

Soon after Roe and I became parents for the first time, she and I and our new son, David, were walking through a church craft fair. We looked at the fancy candles, the quilts, and the sweet jams. At one table a woman was selling toys. David was just an infant, but Roe and I thought that he might like the small green plastic turtle, the yellow bumblebee, and the brown owl with wide eyes. These were finger puppets, but Roe suggested that they would make good bathtub toys for the baby. We bought the turtle, the owl, and the bee at twenty-five cents each, and then we drove home.

Roe was right. The small figures made for terrific bathtub toys, so much so that we began a collection of these little figures: Mickey Mouse, a brown bear, Ernie and Bert from *Sesame Street*. Reaching in for the basket of little toys under the sink became a routine for all of our three children, David, Karen, and Michael, when they bathed in the tub. They liked to line up the creatures along the edge of the tub or on the top of the hot and cold faucets. The children played with the bee and turtle, with Mickey and Bert until the bathwater lost its heat and its entertainment.

Year after year the plastic finger puppets delighted the children, companions out on the open seas of the rough and deep tub at 11 Woodland Court eighty miles west of the Atlantic Ocean.

But children grow up; they find other tools for their imagination. David sought adventure with Matt, the neighbor who likes to play football. Karen goes to the movies with her friend Brittany. What becomes of the little bee and brown owl?

One late evening, when Roe and the children were asleep for the night, I decided to take the garbage out in a final gesture toward order for the day: I reached down for the filled garbage can in the kitchen and was about to carry the pail outside when I noticed an unusual shade of green wedged under a squashed milk carton. I picked the carton up and there, in a jumble of disorder and finality, rested Mickey, Bert and Ernie, the owl, the bee, and the small green turtle. Roe, recognizing that the children had out-grown the finger puppets, threw out the faded, soap-filled, useless toys.

Like a claw in one of those arcade machines, my hand reached down into the trash bin and rescued each figure one by one. After I rinsed each creature in the kitchen sink,

I placed it on the kitchen table until the collection was complete. If the plastic owl could have talked it would have said, "Take us back to the bathroom. Where are the children? We haven't gone out to sea in over a year." Yes, indeed. Where are the children who used the sponge as a raft to sail the bee across the fierce waves to save the turtle, who was being attacked by the soap shark? The house was silent. I gathered up the little creatures into my cupped hands and was about to toss them back into the garbage, but then I slipped the owl onto one of my fingers, wiggled it a bit, then I placed the owl and turtle on my other fingers, and then I slowly walked into the living room.

I decided to keep these plastic toys, my treasures, the little beings that fit between the fingers of my babies.

Knowing that Roe would tease me about my sentimentality, I decided to hide the finger puppets. But where? Behind my books in my writing room? No. Inside my grandfather clock? No. In the basement perhaps. I descended the stairs of the basement like a pirate about to bury his loot. I looked behind the furnace, inside a closet, and under the stairs. Finally, I noticed the hole in the ceiling.

The summer before, Roe and I had hired a company to install a new oil furnace. They removed the old pipes and furnace, and the new heating unit was set in place. But because the new pipes were smaller than the old ones, a hole was left in the basement ceiling. That is where I hid the children's old toys. I carefully placed each character inside the ceiling. I had to push them deep inside so that they could not be seen accidentally. Then I went to bed.

Bert and Ernie, Mickey, bear, turtle, bee, and owl still sit in the darkness of the basement ceiling.

Why do I keep these things hidden in a tight place? Because someday Roe and I will have grandchildren splashing in the tub. The waves will rise. The soap shark will once again seek vengeance, and the sponge raft will carry turtle and the rest to the safety of an old man's open hands, a man who remembers other days, other seas, other waves crashing against his laughing heart. But I kept them for another reason too. They are evidence of God's love, and of a father's love. They are signs on the path to heaven.

II
FAITH

I Love You, and So Does God

For most of us, the path to heaven lies within a community of faith. Christians are brought into this community through the sacrament of baptism, but baptism is not an initiation into an exclusive club. It is the acknowledgment of God's existence in the new child. God is there because others have bequeathed God to the child.

In baptism, we are immersed in water, oil is crossed upon our foreheads, and words are spoken: "I baptize you in the name of the Father, and of the Son, and of the Holy Spirit." I tell my children that for thousands of years people have been baptized like this. I offer this simple ceremony as evidence of heaven's existence. I sometimes think that the ceremony of baptism ought to be accompanied by the jingling of bells and the blowing of trumpets, an announcement of God's presence once more among us.

I was baptized at St. Luke's Church in Waldwick, New Jersey. My godfather is Archbishop Joseph Raya, the former archbishop of Akka, Haifa, Nazareth, and all of Galilee. My godmother is Helen de Vinck, my father's sister. My parents chose as my godparents two people who believe in God's mercy and goodness, who believe that life is difficult and that we must be bold and daring in our love of God. My parents chose two people who did not have any children of their own, who loved children, who loved God, and who were faithful to me.

Every year, my family and I take a vacation in Combermere, Ontario, the site of Madonna House, the Catholic lay apostolate that was founded by Catherine de Hueck Doherty. When we visited last summer, Archbishop Raya was there. The eighty-four-year-old bishop celebrated the

Byzantine liturgy and spoke vigorously about God and love and the unity of faith with those who allow the doors to Christ to be open in their lives. Archbishop Raya is a member of Madonna House. My parents first brought him to Combermere in the early 1960s, when he was a Melchite priest serving the Paterson, New Jersey, church of St. Anne.

As we left Madonna House, Father Raya embraced me and whispered, "I love you, Christopher, and so does God."

Aunt Helen, my godmother, worked for Catholic Charities in Belgium for most of her working life. She never married, but instead devoted her life to raising her brothers and sisters after their mother died young. When her brothers and sisters grew up and started families of their own, she spent her days knitting sweaters and socks for her countless nephews and nieces, listening to their troubles and joys, helping them when she could, and being a presence of stability and goodness in their lives. When she was diagnosed with brain tumors, she underwent many operations, some experimental, to save her life. It was saved. As I write, Helen is in a nursing home in Belgium, enduring the last days of her life with tenderness and faith. She is also eighty-four.

When we arrived home after our nine-hour drive from Canada last summer, I called my mother to tell her that we had arrived safely. She told me that Amoury, my cousin from Belgium, was in America for a medical conference and had brought me a gift from Helen. "She emptied her apartment and has given you her silver-box collection. She wants you to have it."

Helen collected silver pillboxes. Over the years, Roe and I had sent her a few to add to this collection, and now she had given the collection to me. When I received it, there was a note attached from Aunt Helen: "Dear Christopher: I love you, and so does God."

Baptism reminds us all that we are from God and that God loves us from generation to generation. This continuity of faith is part of the spiritual integrity of our hidden life. If we can help others see this true existence of this hidden life, it would make all the difference in the world.

When I was a boy, my grandmother would come into my room each night and say, in Flemish, "A cross and a sleep-well," and then she made a small sign of the cross on my forehead, in the name of the Father, and of the Son, and of the Holy Spirit. See? In the *name,* in God's *name* we baptize each other, as we recognize the noble ancestry of our spiritual selves.

A Match Made in Heaven

In the early 1970s, when I was a graduate student at Columbia University, I fell in love with a woman and dated her for two years. I experienced the plenitude of love. When our hearts are lonely, we will try to fill them with love. I did. I thought we would marry and make a life together. I was wrong. She ended the relationship, saying that she was not in love with me.

I then tasted the loss of love. I was studying literature at the time, and I suddenly understood why the greatest themes in literature involve the loss of love. When we lose love, we rush to fill the void. What does a young man do when the girl he loves does not love him in return? Drink? Inhale cocaine? Seek other women? These make great stories, but they didn't work for me. I never drank or tried any drugs because I didn't want to tamper with my senses; I liked the smell of flowers and the taste of chocolate ice cream. I didn't want to seek another woman for love. Neither did I want to seek women for sex, because I just thought that sex and love ought to be combined like flour and yeast. I wanted God in my loneliness. I wanted that young woman in my life, but I couldn't have her. I knew, somehow, that there was a way to a future, but I didn't know what it was and I couldn't bend my circumstances to my liking by force of will.

So I became a writer. I began to write poetry, and I've been doing it ever since. I fell into it naturally because the rhythms and images of poetry appealed to my somewhat dreamy temperament. I was a boy who liked to find fossils and wildflowers. I was a boy who carried my cat Moses on my shoulder as I collected colorful leaves in the woods behind my parents' house. I was a boy who liked to sit beside a stream and run my fingertips back and forth through the water. Poetry made sense to me.

As we look back at our lives, we can see the patterns of God's guidance. We have choices, and with prayer, we select the way. I tried to select the way of the heart.

I love the scene in Shakespeare's play *Romeo and Juliet* where Friar Lawrence is tending to the herbs in his garden just before Romeo leaps in filled with joy about his newfound love, Juliet. The old monk leans over his garden tending to the herbs, those leaves of magic and healing. If you rub this one against your bruise, it will be cured. If you boil that and drink it, it will soothe. If you chew this stem, it will purify.

I believe God walks in his garden and prunes and plucks and arranges for the healing of those he loves. "I will place this flower of beauty before Chris for two years," says the Lord, "for now Chris is at the age where he seeks the comfort and love of a woman." Perhaps God said, "Chris will love the flower, dream about this flower, court this flower, and because he loves this one flower, he will not seek others. But this is only for a time."

So I loved that young woman and turned away from all other women for two years, and then she left me, deciding that she was not in love with me. The loss of this young woman was one of the greatest moments of suffering I endured in my life. But God was at work in the magic herb garden, tending and arranging.

Becoming a writer wasn't the only thing that happened to me in the aftermath of my sadness. Soon after I lost the young woman I thought I would marry, I met Rosemary, Roe, my Roe. My relationship with my lost love had kept me occupied for two years. If I had not fallen in love with her, I would not have met Roe. I believe that God was keeping me at bay while Roe made her way to my heart. When God plucked the first girl I loved out of the garden of my life, something else had to grow in its place, and that was my writing, my maturity, and Roe. I am who I am today because of Roe and our children and because of my writing, and all were the direct result of my having lost the love of that first woman. At the time, I thought that loss was God's cruelty. It was really God's gift.

When we look back on our lives, we can see the patterns of God's guidance. We are children of God. A true father watches over his children and guides them to grow in wisdom. God must exist. Otherwise, my writing was a fluke. Otherwise, Roe came into my life at random. Otherwise, the birth of our three children was a mere biological event. But I can see the hand of God in these things. I know they were spiritual events, tickets to heaven.

Loretta McSorley and the Stations of the Cross

As I grew older I slowly came to realize that some things about the world were obvious, and some were not so obvious. When I was in seventh grade the world to me was Loretta McSorley. It was obvious that she had crooked teeth, long black hair, and a smile that pleased me. Why that pleased me was not so obvious.

In the early spring of 1962, during Lent, I attended the stations of the cross at my parish, Guardian Angel Church. Perhaps I went more than once, but I only remember this one time, the time of the wooden pews and candles and priest and altar boys and Loretta sitting across the aisle.

As a boy I always suffered along with the story of Jesus as he made his way from being condemned, through his carrying of the cross, and to the final crucifixion. I was especially saddened when Jesus called out from the cross that he was thirsty. I know that much of who I am today comes from the gesture of the soldier dipping his spear into a moist sponge and bringing the sponge to the lips of Jesus so that he could have a small bit of relief.

We cannot escape who we are, and who we are is often formed by the stories we hear, by the heroes we emulate. I wanted to be the soldier who brought water to the lips of Jesus.

I liked the small figures defined for the stations of the cross that encircled the church. I liked sitting in my seat and watching the priest move from station to station, saying the prayers, telling the story. What I liked the most was the opportunity to turn my head and see Loretta. She sat across the aisle and behind me three or four rows back, so it was difficult to see her. I was told by the nuns in my school never to turn around in church, and I never did, except once. I heard a noise in the rear of the church, I turned to look, and an old woman thumped her finger on my head and scowled, "Turn around. Face the front of the church. Where is your respect?" So I never turned my head. But during the stations of the cross that Friday afternoon, I was allowed to turn once the priest made his way to the fifth station because the fifth station was behind me, across the aisle, four rows back. This gave me an excuse to look at Loretta. What surprised me was that she didn't turn around, but instead she looked at me as I turned to look at her, and then she smiled. It is the smile that has stayed with me for forty years, the smile framed in her long black hair. A girl liked me.

It is impossible to exclude the love of a woman in my own spiritual journey. In order to have a spiritual life, we need to find people who define us, who bring us out of ourselves in a way that gives us a new identity. Much of who we are as spiritual people is nurtured by our sensual selves. In order for us to be happy people, we need people who will love us and caress us. Without love, and without such a caress, life becomes tragic.

We cannot discover our spiritual selves in a vacuum. We must react to the external world, and the spiritual side of the external world is in others. My wife and children and my parents define the outline of my spiritual body. Without Roe there would be no Michael or David or Karen. Without Roe there would be no part of me that was defined by Roe, created because of Roe's existence, because of the presence of Roe in my life. Oh yes, it is easy to say if not Roe, then it would have been another woman, but God lead me to Roe.

I believe Roe and I belong to God's plan, and in the plan there is a design that could not be complete otherwise.

But something else stirred in me when Loretta sent me her smile across the aisle during that Friday afternoon Lenten service many years ago. This was an awareness of the interplay between the spiritual and the sensual. The stirring inside of me was a sensual nudge, no doubt, and the sensual part of who we are is closely connected to our spiritual selves. It is impossible for me to explain the part of me that is a writer without understanding that there's a sensual part of being a human being. I did not know about the sensual world until I met Loretta. I didn't know at the time what the feeling was all about, but I now know that I was not just a small boy, but a boy with a secret, and that secret was that I loved Loretta McSorley, and she sent me a smile.

I have been a high school English teacher for twenty-five years, and I have come to understand that great literature is about people who struggle to be loved and caressed. Think of Jay Gatsby. Think of Sydney Carton in *A Tale of Two Cities*. Think of Boo Radley in *To Kill a Mockingbird*. Gatsby just wanted to love Daisy and to be loved by her. Carton wanted to love Lucie Manet and to be loved by her. Boo Radley just wanted to be with the children and be liked by them. These great fictional people longed to be held and loved but were not. If we are not loved and held, we can easily become tragic, or different, or odd, or lonely. Or, perhaps, great heroes and great saints.

Part of the trick of living a happy life is learning how to balance the needs of our spiritual and physical selves. They depend on each other. We need to confidently develop them, exercising the sensual parts of our bodies as well as the spiritual parts of our souls.

If you looked at me as I walked home from church that afternoon, you would have seen an ordinary boy walking along Franklin Turnpike in Allendale, New Jersey, on his way home. You wouldn't have guessed that I had Loretta McSorley inside of me.

We need to share these secret parts of who we are. If we don't, we risk damaging our souls. To grow spiritually, to find our way to heaven, we need the stations of the cross *and* real people in our lives who will nurture our souls and our bodies.

The Virgin in the Window

We are all looking for a path to heaven. In the fall of 2000, Romona and Narcelino Collado said they saw an image of the Virgin Mary of Guadalupe in a window of their second-story apartment at 103 Washington Street, Perth Amboy, New Jersey. Their story sparked local and then national attention, and hundreds of people traveled to the site to sing, pray, stare at the window, and light candles. Police barricades were erected; traffic was diverted. I decided to join them and see the image for myself.

Perth Amboy sits on Raritan Bay at the mouth of the Raritan River. Despite this general geographical certainty, I exited off the Garden State Parkway and quickly realized that I was lost.

I pulled into a tire center, walked inside, and asked a man waiting in line if he could give me directions to Perth Amboy. He was wearing a baseball cap with the words *St. Mary Eagles* embroidered on it in gold thread.

"You going to see the window?" he asked.

"Yes. How did you know?"

"Drive back two miles," he said. "Keep to the right. You'll find State Street, which goes right into Washington."

I thanked the man, drove off, and immediately got lost again. I followed a car with a bumper sticker that read, "God Is Good All the Time." We crossed a small bridge. I was in Perth Amboy. The car with the bumper sticker pulled into a bank, and I continued on my way to the first church I could find, a modest one with a stone statue of the Virgin Mary set among azalea bushes. Soon the parish priest and I were sitting in his office.

"Father, what do you think of the apparition in the window?" I asked him.

"I hear there is a diffuse color in the glass, but no concrete image. Some people tell me that they felt an invisible presence embracing them when they looked up at the window. I can tell you that there is no guarantee that what they see is Our Lady of Guadalupe. I believe the colors in the window are like a Rorschach test, everyone looking at the image and expressing their own personal feelings about what they see. We are limited in our faith by what we see, but not in what we believe."

Before I followed his directions to the house, the priest said, "My people are lovely people. We are mostly Hispanic; many of us are from the Dominican Republic. There are no guarantees." But five minutes later I was lost again. I passed some boys playing stickball, a mother walking with her three children, and two old women wearing colorful kerchiefs over their heads. I saw laundry hanging between buildings, and vegetable stands.

I stopped in at a second church office to ask for directions. (There are nine Catholic churches in Perth Amboy.) "I am interested in the apparition," I said to the kind woman who greeted me.

"Yes, there is much interest. I am a nun working in this parish for three years, and I have never seen anything like this."

"Sister," I asked, "do you think the apparition is real?"

"I went to see for myself," she said. "I didn't see Our Lady's image in the glass. But what moved me was the people's desire to be attuned to God's presence in their lives."

Ten minutes later, I stood before 103 Washington Street, a modest two-story house: the bottom facade made of brick, the top half covered in yellow siding. Approximately eighty people were standing on the sidewalk, looking up at the third window to the left.

There was a swirled, diffuse color in the glass, making it look as if there were a defect embedded in it. Hundreds of candles had been placed on the pavement in front of the house. People were walking inside the apartment in order to get a closer look at the window. I watched from the sidewalk as children on the other side of the window followed their mother's careful instruction to touch the glass gently. An old man placed his wrinkled hand on the glass and tapped three times with his fingers. Teenage girls whispered when they stroked the windowpane.

I asked a policeman behind the barricade what he thought about the apparition. "I've been on duty here for the past three days, and I don't see anything in the window," he said. A woman beside me said to a child, "Go light a candle for your grandfather."

Like my son Michael, the people of Perth Amboy were seeking evidence of heaven. They understood that proof of its existence would make all the difference in the world. But the evidence of God's existence was not embedded in the upstairs window; it was in the hearts of all the thousands of people who came to it with great faith. While we may never find proof of the existence of heaven, we keep searching, and we keep believing, because we have faith.

We are driven by our hunger for God. Michael feels the urge to seek out God's existence. The people of Perth Amboy felt compelled to take a look for themselves at the color in the glass. This inner urgency to seek God is God speaking directly to us. If we listen closely, we will find our way home.

Faith of a Poet

I began writing poetry in the winter of 1974. Over the years, I have tried to explain why. I would say I liked to read, or my mother was a writer, or I was lonely, or that it was a natural thing for a student and teacher of English to do. But I knew, all along, that my urge to write was God's will. I wrote poetry because God made me this way. My friend Fred Rogers helped me realize this. He was open with his faith, so free to speak about God, as if God was right there beside us as we spoke, that I slowly learned to become comfortable with seeing God, the Holy Spirit, a vocation, and holiness in connection with my writing.

I have in my desk drawer more than a thousand poems I have written during the past twenty-six years. Very few of them have been published. When this depresses me, I think of Emily Dickinson, who published hardly any poems in her lifetime. After she wrote a poem, she would slip it into her desk drawer, and that was that. So I continue doing the same, knowing full well that meager publishing is about the only thing I have in common with that great poet.

Well, there's one other thing. Emily Dickinson kept writing because she felt compelled to do so. I, and many other poets and writers, are the same. It is what we feel we have to do. From where does this impulse arise? I believe that, for me, it comes from the presence of God deep inside me. The writing is guided in some mysterious fashion by the Holy Spirit. When I began to write in 1974, I made a promise to myself that I would strive for beauty in my work. I promised myself that I would not write about ugliness, suicide, violence, or evil. Rather, I would write about gracefulness, gentleness, goodness. I do not dismiss the dark side of human existence. My poetry is filled with sorrow and loss and death and ugliness, but not to celebrate these things. Instead, they affirm the truth that even after the darkest nights, joy does, indeed, come in the morning.

The same goal drives my teaching. I once thought that I became a high school teacher because I wanted to teach children the basic skills of reading and writing. I now know that I became a teacher because I wanted children to recognize that God exists within them and that one way to discover this truth is to read writers like T. S. Eliot, Mary Oliver, Toni Morrison, Archibald MacLeish, and William Carlos Williams.

I am a writer because God made me a writer. What I write is for the glory of God. I write to add my voice to the voices of all people of faith who say, aloud, there is a heaven, God exists, life is difficult, but God is good. Yes, we are often tired, defeated, lonely, angry, but God is there to comfort us, to feed us, to love us unconditionally. I write poetry because I need to express, overtly, that heaven is real. I hope there is evidence of God, beauty, passion, and paradise in all that I write.

When we are close to our own dying, when the sun of our lives begins its final descent, what happens? I know what happens: a light appears, a gold light perhaps, like honey. It is the light of heaven.

The light of God is much brighter than our simple notions of light. It is brighter than the light we know here on earth. Yet we fear the loss of the old light, the light of our earthly lives. Do not, I say in my poetry, fear the loss of this old light, for beyond the light lies the ocean of God's love, and sitting by the fireside in heaven is God, waiting for us.

III
FAMILY

The Swoon of Faith

Some people agonize all their lives as they search for evidence of faith, or God, or salvation. Others simply disbelieve such things. My friend Henri Nouwen taught at Harvard for a while. He preached loudly and with certitude that there is a God and a heaven and a merciful Christ and a joyous church and great forgiveness and the celebration of God's love in each day. Henri was an easy target for the scholars and intellectuals. They laughed at his innocent vision and his joyous heart.

I have come to my faith in a simpler way. I came to my own faith long before I could read, long before I attended Catholic school or Mass. I believe in the existence of heaven and in God because my mother told me it was true. It was as simple as that.

My mother would not lie to me. When I was a child, she pointed out the moon to me. She held kittens in her hands and had me listen to the extraordinary sound of their hearts beating. She was right about those things, so I believed her when she told me about Jesus. Jesus promised us that there was a heaven, and my mother told me about that promise. So I believed.

But when that early certitude of faith began to wane, I trusted in companions and signs to bring me back. I'm like Hansel and Gretel, who dropped stones along the way into the forest so they could find the way home. I'm like an old sailor, looking to the stars for guidance across the great seas. God places little stones for us to follow through the dark woods of life. God places certain stars in our hearts so that we can take a measured reading and determine where we are when we feel lost.

For sure, times will come when we feel lost. At each step along the way to God, dark shadows, walls, deep forests, and traps lie in our way and tempt us with distractions. Is this the devil's work? The closer we come to a purity of heart, the harder the devil seems to work to dissuade us. The closer we come to opening the next door to God's love, the more we see false passageways and ladders made of straw. We hear songs that lead us to dash our brains against the jutting rocks of a ragged shore of delusion. We need good reasons to choose the doors carefully, choose the right companions, choose with care the partner we will embrace along the way.

As a child, I began to acquire an inner desire to imitate those I loved. This desire came naturally as my spirit awakened, as I slowly became aware of the crows and daylilies, when I was able to name my father and grandfather, when I reached an age where I could delight in a chocolate ice-cream cone and catch pollywogs in the spring pool. We are driven to imitate. Child psychologists and linguists might explain how a child learns language: by imitating the exclusive sounds they hear over and over again. But they can't explain where the urge to imitate comes from. We like to imitate each other. We want to be like those movie stars, or like our father, or like our teachers. We look to people for hints of how we want to dress, eat, talk, and how to love.

For me, the stars I look to for guidance are the people I love. As a child, I picked up mannerisms, habits, delights from those who surrounded me. I watched my family closely and learned from them, even imitating them at times. When my grandfather, who was a general in the Belgian army, was outside tending to his glorious rose garden, I was inside, secretly trying on his general's cap in his bedroom. When my father shaved, I watched carefully, and then I too pulled the skin on my face taut and shaved with my plastic shaving kit, made for serious little boys who wanted to look fine and handsome. From my mother, I learned about receiving communion.

Many years before I received my first communion, I was in church with my parents and sisters and brothers. I remember watching my mother walk up to the front of the church to receive the Eucharist. When she came back to the pew, she took off her glasses, placed her face into her open, cupped hands, and knelt in a still silence.

Then, after a few moments, she fainted in my father's arms.

My mother would often swoon after communion. When she was revived from her unconscious state, she would frequently have tears in her eyes, but she would always be smiling. I often smiled back at her, as if she had gone off on a trip and now was back. I knew that wherever she had gone, it was a good place. Communion was exceptionally important to my mother, and it became important to me too. I never fainted after receiving the Bread of Life, but it affects me deeply each time I receive it because it reminds me of my mother's promise—and Christ's promise—that heaven exists.

My faith grew stronger, in part, because of what I observed in my mother. I wanted to be like her. She believed in love and hope, and she received these things every Sunday, in the form of a small piece of bread. "The future of humanity lies in the hands of those who are strong enough to provide coming generations with reasons for loving and hoping."

Holy Communion is like the stones in the woods and the stars in the night; it is a guidepost on the path to heaven.

Every time we eat the bread and drink the wine, we can get a hint of God, but for me it is only a hint. It has something to do with the pebbles along the path or the stars that guide the sailor on the seas. Jesus asked that we bless the bread and wine in his memory. We read and reread a letter from a loved one to conjure up the memory of that person, and if we think hard enough, that person is almost present before us. Perhaps the Eucharist, the child's bread, is the best evidence of the restorative powers of God's love.

In this world filled with doubt, I take my son to church on Sundays, and I tell him there is a glorious heaven, a merciful God, a playful Christ, a small heartbeat deep inside the kitten's chest. I tell him about the Eucharist. I am Hansel dropping stones of faith along the way for my three children. I scoop up the memories of my mother's love for God and scatter them above their heads in the night sky, creating a Milky Way of faith. I do this just as Jesus scattered his stars and pebbles in the form of broken bread and blessed wine, so that we may follow him.

My Father's Rosary

Before I made my first Holy Communion, I had to take a class to learn about the sacrament. The nuns prepared my little class with catechisms and rehearsals. I remember kneeling at the wooden altar rail as Sister, pretending she was the host-giving priest, came to each of us and tapped our extended tongues with the closed point of her pen, at which point we were supposed to say, "Amen."

At the end of our training, Sister announced that we could purchase the Holy Communion packet: a white purse, a white Bible, and white rosary beads for the girls; a tie, a black Bible, and black rosary beads for the boys. Then she asked us to raise our hands if we wanted to place an order.

I had never, in all my seven years, made a financial decision, so I didn't raise my hand.

On the day of my first communion, after all the rush and fuss, I found myself squeezed into a pew inside the church. We boys sat on the left side of the church while the girls sat on the right. There was just enough room for the parents to sit behind us, at the rear of the church.

The parish priest began the ceremonies with a general blessing, and then he asked all the children to lift their Bibles to be blessed.

I looked around and watched all the kids in the church raise their little white and black Bibles above their heads. I was the only one without a Bible. I felt out of place and lonely.

Then the priest asked us to lift our rosary beads. Again, everyone did as the priest asked. I would have to endure the embarrassment twice.

But just before the blessing, there was a disturbance at the rear of the church. I turned to look with everyone else. Someone was squeezing past the cramped people in his pew, trying to leave his seat in the middle. Then I saw that the person was my father. He excused himself one more time before stepping out into the aisle.

The ceremony stopped. The priest lowered his hands. The children, one by one, lowered their rosary beads.

My father walked purposefully to the front of the church, reached into his pocket, pulled out his long, brown rosary beads, leaned over the pew, stretched his long arm in my direction, and handed me his rosary beads. Then he smiled. I smiled back.

He quickly returned to his seat as the priest announced, with understanding, "Could you *all* please lift your beads for the blessing?"

That day I made a significant discovery about myself as a spiritual creature. From before I was born, to my own birth, to that moment in the church, my father had reached out across time and space and extended his love, his faith, and his rosary beads to his son. He reached out and led me out of my loneliness, inviting me back into the community of faith.

Each time we go to church and recite the ancient prayers, we repeat hints of God that have been delivered to us by our fathers and forefathers. This is tradition. When we surround ourselves with the traditions of faith, we become part of a community that lives under God's love. We feel less alone in such a community, less frightened. In the traditions of our faith, we feel a certain expectation for the future, and the more we believe in God's love, the more we believe in the certitude of those expectations. God's love is manifested in ancient ritual, in prayer, in the actions of the father. God reaches out to us from across the pew and hands us beads, tokens of his love, assurance that we are not alone. Heaven beckons.

The Miracle of the Prayer Cards

In the final months of World War II, my grandfather, an officer in the Belgian army, received word that he was to report to Paris to participate in the task of rebuilding Europe. My mother, who was twenty at the time, anxiously asked my grandfather if she could join him.

Belgium, like the rest of Europe, had endured four years of Nazi occupation. My mother had spent half of her teenage life under the banner of the swastika, living with curfews, bombings, and starvation. Every few weeks, the Gestapo would knock on the front door of my grandmother's house, always with the same question: "Where is the colonel?" At the outbreak of the war, the Germans pushed my grandfather out of Belgium and chased him across the southern portion of the vulnerable continent. He managed to escape to Spain, where he was captured and sent to prison. Released in a prisoner exchange, he was sent to England, where he worked for the European underground to foil Hitler's madness.

No wonder my mother was eager to join her father on a trip to Paris. She hadn't been beyond her street corner in four years. She tells us today that the first white bread she ate in four years was at the American canteen, where she also had fresh milk and real chocolate.

"Absolutely not," my grandfather said. "I will be in France on official military business. I will not have time to take care of you."

"But," my mother protested, "you don't have to take care of me. I can read and walk and just be free."

"It is no place for a young woman, and I repeat, my work is for people in uniform only."

My grandmother looked at my mother's eyes, stepped out of the room, and returned a few moments later, holding up one of my grandfather's old uniforms. "What if she goes in this?"

"That's a great idea," my mother said as she walked around the uniform, examining it.

"Impossible," my grandfather said. "It is too big, and there are no women in the army. Ridiculous."

"But I can sew the uniform, tuck it in here and here and cut a little here, and she could wear one of your old caps," my grandmother said.

"And I would not get in your way. I would stand behind you wherever you went," my mother added.

My grandfather looked at the uniform, at my grand-mother, at my mother. Then he smiled and said, "All right. I see I will have a military aide joining me on my trip to Paris."

And so my mother went to Paris, with nothing more than her wallet, her uniform, a simple skirt and blouse, and her father at her side.

In November 1944, they arrived in Paris, a gloomy, cold, and recently liberated city that had been worn down by war and hunger. There was no heat in the city, for all the coal and oil had been taken by the Nazi troops for their war efforts.

My mother spent those first nights with my grandfather in the Hotel du Garage Citroen, which, of course, had no heat. My mother said that she was so cold at night that she would pick up the small carpet off the floor and stretch it upon her, adding it to her bedcovers. For the first few days, my mother and grandfather walked through the streets of Paris simply to stay warm. The Battle of the Bulge was still one month away.

On the fifth day after their arrival, my grandfather and mother greeted a Belgian officer who was to work with my grandfather to set up a way to help people return to Belgium at the end of the war. This Belgian, Alfred Cruysmans, had an assistant with him by the name of Jose de Vinck, who wanted to join him on this trip so that he could try to sell an edition of the Gospels that he had published.

Because Mr. Cruysmans and my grandfather were both officers, they were allowed to eat at the American canteen, where there was heat and food. Of course, my mother was not allowed to go with them, so Mr. Cruysmans asked Jose de Vinck to take her to breakfast. This would be a difficult task, because there wasn't much food to be found in Paris and because my father was thirty years old and didn't want anything to do with the colonel's twenty-year-old child. But Jose's boss probably coerced him, and so the colonel's daughter and the Gospel salesman found a small café, where they ordered chicory coffee, a drink they had never before tasted.

After their glamorous breakfast, they decided to walk along the Seine, where the sellers of used books displayed their wares. As my mother and her companion began to browse through the stacks of old books, they noticed that they wanted to buy the same books, so they came up with a system: my mother would get one, and then her companion would get one, and so on. But then they came upon the works of Angela of Foligno, an Italian mystic of the Middle Ages, and they both wanted the book. After some polite banter, Jose jokingly said that the only solution was to get married so that they could have joint custody of the volume. They bought the book together.

As they walked along the riverbank, Jose suddenly said, "I always carry a prayer by Cardinal Mercier. It is called 'Prayer to the Holy Spirit.'" He pulled a small prayer card out of his wallet and read aloud:

O Holy Spirit, soul of my soul, I adore thee.
Guide me, strengthen me, console me,
Tell me what to do, give me thy orders,
And I promise to submit
To whatever thou desirest of me,
And to accept everything
Thou allowest to happen to me.
Let me know thy will.

After Jose finished reading this prayer, he slipped the card back into his wallet. And then my mother opened her purse, pulled a prayer card out of *her* wallet, and read aloud:

O Holy Spirit, soul of my soul, I adore thee.
Guide me, strengthen me, console me,
Tell me what to do, give me thy orders,
And I promise to submit
To whatever thou desirest of me,
And to accept everything
Thou allowest to happen to me.
Let me know thy will.

Three days later, after my mother and father prayed together before the statue of our Lady in Notre Dame Cathedral, they decided to get married. They married two months later in Brussels.

The moment of my parents' meeting has enormous significance, because it was also the moment of my spiritual conception. I can trace back part of my own beginnings to the spiritual union of my mother and father on that cold morning in November 1944 when they shared the cardinal's prayer.

We are all born of a historical union between a man and a woman. But we are also born because of a near incalculable number of people who were born before us. We are the sons and daughters of our parents, but we are also the children of two sets of grandparents, four sets of great-grandparents, and on and on. I suspect that most of us are born out of love, physically and spiritually created from the union of millions of people. The poet Walt Whitman said that perhaps the soul is the combination of all people. We are related to each other not only by the evidence of DNA, but also by the evidence of love. Millions of people had to love each other and love their children in order for our own births to occur.

This is the story. It was told before the invention of the printing press, and parchment, and pens and tablets, and carving tools, the word passed on from parents to children and so to the next parents and so to the next children. It is the tangible evidence of a spiritual existence. But we risk losing sight of the original drama as we adorn our lives with symbols that attempt to divine our way back to God. Our spiritual past is more rooted in the poet's voice than in DNA research and other scientific studies of our physical history.

We are a nation divided on the issue of life. When does it begin? When should it be preserved? Scientists and doctors and politicians argue, pinpoint, offer opinions, and research, all in an attempt to claim that they have discovered the exact moment when human life begins. But what of the perpetual spiritual life that was born back in the time of God's loneliness? The life of each child began millions of years ago.

I am intrigued by physical evidence that the human body existed millions of years ago. But I am much more intrigued by the fact that my mother and father carried identical prayer cards and recited them to each other on a cold morning in Paris in 1944. My mother recently found the two cards in a drawer. They are evidence of God's existence, of that God-whisper, that God-trace, that holy version of us that exists beyond the physical reality of our bodies.

Of his prayer, Cardinal Mercier said, "I will reveal to you a secret of sanctity and of happiness: if every day, during five minutes, you are able to quiet your imagination, to close your eyes to the things of the senses, and your ears to the rumors of the earth, to enter within yourself, and there, in the sanctuary of your baptized soul, which is the temple of the Holy Spirit, thus to speak to this Divine Spirit, if you do this, your life will flow happily, serene and consoled, even in the midst of pain, for grace will be proportioned to the trial, giving you the strength to bear it; and loaded with merits, you will reach the gates of paradise."

This is a fact that is more true than science. We might be physically constructed with DNA strands weaving among themselves, but we are spiritually constructed with strands of grace connected to each other in ways far more binding than DNA. According to the *New York Times,* scientists are thrilled that the prehistoric skulls in Georgia "linked them to the early human species who lived from 1.9 million to 1.4 million years ago and who some researchers think is the African version of Homo erectus." I am more impressed that Neanderthal man liked flowers.

The way to heaven lies in these spiritual places beyond the things of our senses, that place between the music of Mozart and our hearing, that place between the writer and the blank page, that place where the spiritual side of us responds to the Eucharist. Walt Whitman asked, "What is it then between us? What is the count of the scores or hundreds of years between us?" Love is between us.

The moment my mother began reading the duplicate prayer to my father, they recognized what it was, indeed, that they had between them. My mother said that she did not fall in love with my father in a Hollywood fantasy way. Instead, she had a strong sense of destiny, a moisture of certitude that my father was to be her husband, that their union had been ordained from the very beginning of eternity. My mother felt the condition of the Holy Spirit that already existed in the world.

Old Man Christmas

In Poland, the midnight Mass on Christmas Eve is called Pasterka, "the Mass of the Shepherds." It is said that after the Mass, on Christmas Day, those who have maintained a purity of heart for the whole year might see a path to heaven open up on the winter horizon.

An old Polish grandfather told me about this when I was a boy. His name was Josh. He lived next door to us in a bungalow that sat beside a small field, good for cabbage in the summer and snowball fights in the winter. The old man's face looked like wrinkled caramel, brown and woodlike. His fingers were thick. He wore black boots with metal clasps, a red-and-black-checkered coat. I watched him collect white eggs in his chicken coop and noticed that he did so as if he were lifting blown glass from the shelves at Tiffany's.

Josh seemed gruff, and he didn't speak English well, but he liked my sister and me. Around Christmastime, if there was snow on the ground, we would go sledding on the hill that ran from his property to the main road. When he saw us coming, he would laugh and point to the hill. "Go down," he'd say. "Go down." His great smile revealed the gaps between his teeth.

Not many people believe that you can see a path to heaven on Christmas Day. We do not live in a culture that celebrates God's promise that we will return to the Father with our complete bodies and souls and live forever in a kingdom of goodness and love and peace. People are cynical about heaven and skeptical about goodness. When I say to my students that people are basically good, they laugh. When I tell sophisticated friends about my belief in heaven, they frown and change the subject. The everyday messages of goodness, hope, God, and heaven are drowned out by images of violence and words of doubt. These days, cynicism even reigns at Christmas, as I discovered during a little journey I took in my neighborhood.

When David was eight, Karen was five, and Michael was three, I had a Santa Claus suit made for me. I have played Santa every year since then. On Christmas Eve, I go up into the attic and retrieve the suit. I tuck my black hair under the white wig, stuff a pillow into the waist of the baggy red pants, tighten the black belt around the red coat, and adjust the stocking cap on my head. Then I set forth through the neighborhood, waving at the neighbors. One year, the children joined me as I walked around the neighborhood, ringing a bell.

But last Christmas Eve, no one wanted to join me on my tour of the neighborhood. I carried on nevertheless. I got out the Santa suit, looped the white beard around my face, put on the stovepipe pants, and adjusted the wire-rimmed glasses that sat on the end of my nose. I whispered, "Ho, ho, ho" as I admired myself in the mirror. "Ho, ho, ho!" I bellowed as I walked down the stairs and into the family room. "Who wants to walk around the court with Santa?"

My three teenagers rolled their eyes.

Alone, I stepped outside the house in my Santa Claus suit. "Merry Christmas," I said into the darkness. I hoped the neighborhood children would inadvertently look out their windows and come out to join me. They didn't.

When I was halfway around the court, a car approached. It crept slowly by as a man rolled down his window and shouted, "How the hell you doin', Santa?" Then he threw an empty beer can at me. As the car sped away, I saw no path to heaven, but two fading red lights bouncing in the darkness.

It was enough to discourage the hardiest fan of Christmas. But I will persevere. Despite the beer can and my children's lost interest in Santa Claus, I still believe that this is a Jimmy Stewart wonderful life and that Scrooge will always raise Bob Cratchit's salary.

Let us light candles, exchange gifts, drive home tired children at the end of Christmas day. Let us consider our own regrets and flawed victories and still believe there is a hill for sledding, an old man placing white eggs into our warm hands, and a small opening in the sky for Jacob's ladder, the ascent into heaven.

IV
IMAGINATION

Creating and Loving

Creativity is one of the paths to heaven. When my son Michael imagined the old man living in Australia, he was following a creative impulse. We invent things in our imaginations and create music, poetry, and sculpture to end our loneliness, to express love, to develop a sense of permanence in an impermanent world. The creative act builds a bridge from a point of ugliness to a point of beauty. Michael wanted knowledge of heaven's beauty, so he built a bridge.

Creative work is always joyous, no matter how much work it takes—and it does take work. We build a path to heaven one stone at a time, just as God built the church one stone at a time. And just as God's building the church was an expression of God's love, our building of churches around the world is a creative expression of our love, faith, and spiritual history.

Churches are places of worship, but they are also expressions of the joy that is inherent in the creative process of building. While I prefer the beauty of a church made of wood from the local forests, I also delight in the beauty of Notre Dame in Paris, of St. Peter's Basilica in Rome, and, especially, of St. Patrick's Cathedral in New York. This cathedral was built in the Gothic style: its ornate spires shoot upward, expressing the flamboyance and verve that Gothic architects felt as they soared beyond the cumbersome and formal Romanesque architectural style. When I think of Romanesque architecture, I think of a turtle. When I think of the Gothic style, I think of a stork.

When I think of building churches, I am reminded of my own attempt at building something for the glory of God: the church I built for my mother when I was a child.

I built the church in the basement of the house where I grew up. My memory of this is one of the very first to attach itself to the notion of God—that there is something beyond the house and woods and distant train whistles. I knew as a child that religion was important to my mother and father, though I didn't call it religion. We attended mass on Sundays. I liked the smell of the incense and noticed how all the women in the choir looked like the Old Maid card. I liked how our pastor began each sermon year after year with the words, "My dear friends." My mother kept a photograph in her kitchen of St. Theresa, and my father had hung the image of the Shroud of Turin on the wall. Dried palms were wedged behind Dali's painting of Christ's crucifixion. I considered the church to be the center of the holy celebration that my parents seemed to enjoy so much. Little did I know then how liturgically correct I was.

My mother was to have a birthday on February 20, and I decided to build her a church as a gift. I cannot understand today why exactly I did this. What would a mother do with her very own church?

One afternoon I walked down the winding steps to the basement. I found what I needed at my father's workbench: wood, a saw, and glue. My church needed walls, so I found a thin piece of plywood about ten inches wide and ten inches high. I cut off the corners on one end with my father's saw so that the piece of wood looked like the profile of a house. Then I found a heavy piece of wood that was about a half-inch thick and as wide and long as a book. This was the base of my church. I nailed the plywood profile to the base, and I had what looked like a church. With a purple crayon I drew windows on the flat piece of wood that was the front of the church. Then I glued onto the base a small rectangular piece of wood that looked to me like a tiny altar. I found a long piece of scrap wood and glued that to my church, making what I thought looked like a pew. To finish it off, I drew a cross on the peak of the front panel.

I worked for three days to build my mother's church. Each afternoon when I felt I had done enough work, I hid my church under the workbench, behind a box of tools. Lying in bed each night, I thought about how happy my mother was going to be to have her own church.

On the day of her birthday, I ran down to the basement, reached behind the toolbox, and presented the gift to my mother. I do not remember her reaction. Nor do I remember what happened to the little church. My mother doesn't even remember that I presented her with such a thing, and my mother remembers almost everything. But I remember how it felt to cut the wood. I remember thinking how important God was and how important my mother was. I remember the smell of the dampness in the basement and fearing the furnace whenever it roared. I remember how it felt to hammer the nails into the wood, and I remember the delight I felt at finding the purple crayon and drawing what I thought were perfect church windows.

When I look at the windows of St. Peter's in Rome, or the gargoyles of Notre Dame, or the simple statue of Mary at our own local church, I think of the unknown craftspeople who spent their lives working on the construction of our great churches. I feel a connection to them, a bond in creativity.

One of my favorite films is *Lilies of the Field,* a story about a group of German nuns living in the southwestern United States who try to build a church for the local poor. They have no money. They can hardly speak English. The only thing they have is their faith, which manifests itself in the arrival of Homer Smith, who happens to be passing through town. The good nuns, through their innocence and prayers, convince Mr. Smith to build a chapel. It is a story of creating something for the glory of God.

That movie was the very first film to create a spiritual jolt inside of me. I was twelve when I saw it. I liked Homer Smith. I liked how stubborn he was. He wanted to build the church on his own, and yet when he finally gave in to his exhaustion, the people in the town were able to pitch in. I understand the joy Homer Smith felt when he wrote his name in the wet cement at the base of the steeple's cross. For the glory of God, we build this church. For the glory of God, we build upon this rock. For the love of a mother, the child hunts for the purple crayon and draws his church windows. We build things to make connections with those we love.

During a sermon Cardinal Spellman delivered at St. Patrick's in May 1942, he said about the cathedral, "At its portals, the world seems left behind and every advancing step brings heaven nearer and deepens the soul's union with divinity." The church is one beginning of the true path to heaven, and I sensed that as a child when I built that little church.

I was happy when I built that church for my mother. I learned later that happiness was the expression of the flamboyance associated with the Gothic tradition of architecture. Indeed, I later learned that creative work produces an inner happiness that expresses what is flamboyant and instinctive in us all. Beginning with that early time, I learned to trust the surge of delight that accompanies the act of creation.

We ought to trust our creative urges. They are an attempt to express our spiritual selves, and our spiritual selves lead us to God. The more we trust our creative urges, the easier the path to heaven is to see.

Halloween Light

One October morning I stepped out from my bedroom and stood under the pull-down stairs that are cut out in the hall ceiling. I reached up, grabbed the rope and pulled. The wood stairs unfolded, clicked into place, and then I climbed into the attic. I smelled the dust and cool air as I reached the top of the stairs. I gazed on suitcases, the children's old stuffed animals, wrapping paper, Christmas boxes, a crib, forgotten letters, somewhere a wedding gown and a blue suit. Then I found the pumpkin, a significant artifact from my little heaven here at home.

For many years I said how I'd like a glowing pumpkin to place at the front window during the Halloween season. Finally, Roe bought me an orange plastic pumpkin with an electric cord and a small light bulb. During the first week of October, I retrieve my pumpkin from the attic, and then I search in the basement for the tall, narrow, wood table that I use for my pumpkin's perch. The table is not quite tall enough, so each autumn I pull out three books from my shelf to add the extra height needed so that the children in the neighborhood can see the illuminated face of my jack-o'-lantern. This year I chose a biography of William Faulkner, *The Collected Poems of May Sarton,* and the letters of Wallace Stevens.

In a letter dated October 26, 1942, Stevens wrote to his daughter to convince her to stay in college. He said, "Hold on where you are above everything else. Learn to live the good in your heart." When we are born, God sends us a birthday card which reads, "Live the good in your heart." Perhaps this is the message the old Australian could send back to Michael as he struggles with his questions of faith.

The biography of William Faulkner contains an account of an interview he gave in 1931 when he was writing *Light in August.* He said, "There is the stage when you believe everything and everybody is good. Then there is the second, cynical stage when you believe that no one is good. Then at last you come to realize that everyone is capable of almost anything—heroism or cowardice, tenderness or cruelty." We who are heroic and tender will have an easier trip to heaven.

In one of my favorite poems by May Sarton, *Autumn Sonnets,* she wrote, "This open self must grow more harsh and strange / Before it meets the softness of the snow. / Withstand, endure, the worst is still to come." May was a friend of mine, and she suffered greatly throughout her life and understood sorrow, and yet she also understood the softness of self and she had great faith that God and heaven existed.

The goodness in our hearts, heroism and tenderness, the faith to endure—these were the things spoken of in the books that lifted my pumpkin to the windowsill that year.

As I carried my pumpkin down from the attic, I held it against my stomach and imagined what it was like for Roe to carry our unborn children one by one, the round, bulging evidence of a life on his or her way.

We are all capable of cruelty and tenderness; we often feel that we are becoming harsh and strange, but if we look, we will find the glowing good in our hearts—the light that comes from God. It is the light that illuminates the road to heaven.

I Am the Music

L ate last fall, I found what might have been the last cricket in New Jersey. As I raked the autumn leaves, I was sure that I heard a cricket. Cricket sounds are one of the constants in my life. Ever since I was a child, I have loved the music of the cricket, the soothing "ricket, ricket" song in late autumn, when the apples are formed and the pumpkins are round like little Buddhas.

When I stopped raking, the small, distant noise stopped too. I held the rake in my hands, the autumn soldier ready for duty. I shouldered the rake and stepped to the edge of the house, and then I stood still.

"Ricket. Ricket."

I found my cricket sitting in the center of a flat gray stone in the weak heat of the November sun. *What do you have to celebrate?* I said to myself as I looked at the tiny insect, thinking of the coming snow and cold. This small black creature would soon slip between the cracks in the foundation of the house or crawl under the rock and close itself down in the silent dark to await new life in the spring. I sympathized. I sometimes want to crawl into a dark place, curl up for a long time, and push out thoughts of the day's heat, the past's cold memories, the moment's dread. But I'm rescued by memories of the songs my grandmother sang at church or of the songs Roe hums when we are working in the yard.

"Ricket. Ricket. Ricket."

I placed the rake on the ground and knelt down. God listens to me as I sing a lament. God sees my times of loneliness. God does not abandon me. When I feel defeat lingering in the cold air and falling leaves, there is always the promise of spring. I have toiled my way through spring and summer. I can see the fruits of my planting: children growing, wife at ease with the world, books written, students taught. I feel connected, safe.

But the struggle is always there. To live in this temporal world is difficult enough; to try to live side by side with a spiritual self adds to the confusion. I try to nurture what grows around me—my family, my friends, my students—but inside me, a nagging self demands attention. I am often torn between selfishness and selflessness: both seem to hurt, and yet I recognize that this inner struggle is the battle for my soul.

Avoiding myself and avoiding others creates a hollow sound inside my heart. Tending to myself and to others as best I can creates pleasure and victories, which will ultimately lead me to heaven. My mother promised me. Jesus promised me. This is what I can promise Michael. But finding the balance is tricky. If I spend too much effort trying to please myself, I feel guilty. If I spend too much effort tending to others, I am exhausted and at the brink of ruin.

During my first year teaching, I rented a basement apartment from a man who spent his life playing the violin and teaching the violin. At the end of my first month in my little home, I found a note in my mailbox. It was from my landlord's wife inviting me to an evening concert performed by her husband.

After my TV dinner, I walked out of my apartment, followed a small path to the front door of the house and knocked. The door opened, and there was my landlord, dressed in a suit. He smiled, welcomed me into his home. His wife sat on the couch; a music stand stood in the middle of the room. He directed me to sit beside his wife.

I sat down. The man reached behind the couch and pulled out a violin. He smiled, stepped up to the silver music stand and said, "I will play for you this evening a bit of Mozart and Bach." He then placed the violin under his chin, lifted the bow and began to weave a weeping sound of passion. Slow and beautiful. Slow and beautiful. He played for twenty minutes. When he stopped, the house was silent.

Later that evening, his wife spread out various newspaper clippings of her husband's concerts and little awards received at local events. She gave me lemon cake and tea. I then thanked them for the pleasant evening. As he escorted me to the door, the man looked at me and said, "I am the music sometimes."

Perhaps the balance for me is in the music. I am the music—the sound I make as a father and husband and teacher and writer. I am a man with faith, or a faithful man who demands too much of faith.

My landlord never played for me again. He and his wife died long ago. As I sat beside my cricket, I thought of the violin player. We play the music, and then the silence. We are sometimes the music, and then the silence. The cold restricts our movements, restricts the joints in our bones, but then we become elastic and nimble again in heaven.

Plaster-of-Paris Sacrament

We cherish physical evidence of the spiritual realm. Things we can see and touch help us believe. We reverence relics, holy cards, statues of the saints. We bless ourselves with holy water, eat bread and drink wine in church, light candles. This is our sacramental imagination at work—our restless desire to make the spiritual concrete.

This is why I became a writer of poetry. Poetry is one of the most powerful ways to find hints of a spiritual world. Poetry gives us metaphors for the substance of the human soul. T. S. Eliot was a lonely man who suspected that his life had been meaningless, and yet he was filled with a fire for beauty that yielded such sacramental gems as "The Love Song of J. Alfred Prufrock." Robert Frost recognized the similarities between a rural life and the ravishes the human soul endures in its own seasons. He joined the two in "Birches," "Spring Pools," "Death of the Hired Man."

Some people doubt that there's convincing physical evidence of our spiritual selves. I know they're wrong. I don't have to look any farther than the little statue that has been sitting on a shelf in my mother's kitchen for forty years. It shows me that God is indeed inside us.

In the summer of 1961, my sister Anne and I signed up for our church summer-school program. She was twelve and smart. I was ten and goofy. The summer-school program lasted for two weeks and ran from nine in the morning to noon. It was located in a renovated barn on the church's property and was mostly an arts-and-crafts program.

Each day began with a simple prayer, led by one of the two teenage girls who organized the activities. We spent those summer mornings making stained-glass collages of

Bible stories, clay figures of the saints, Popsicle-stick boxes. One day we made plaster-of-paris molds. I liked this activity the best. To this day, one of my favorite aromas is the smell of plaster of paris. The white powder comes in a thick red paper bag. Working with the plaster of paris made me think that I was an artist, and a sort-of baker.

Pamela, the teenage counselor with long braids, demonstrated the activity for the day, and Anne and I followed her every move. We scooped the powder into our small sand pails, slowly poured water into the pails, and stirred it with a wooden mixing spoon. The white powder began to thicken, just as Pamela said it would.

"Now," Pamela said, "I am going to pass out a box filled with different molds. You will each get to select one."

When the box was passed to me, I looked inside and saw a bunch of odd-shaped rubber objects. I pulled one out of the box and held it in my hands. It looked vaguely like a statue of someone.

"Look inside the mold, Christopher," Pamela said.

I turned the rubber mold upside down and looked inside. There I could see the clear figure of a man.

"Chrissy," Anne said, "don't you get it? We pour the plaster of paris into the mold, let it harden, and then we pull off the rubber and the statue is made. See? The inside part of the rubber has the impression of the statue. It's like a cookie mold."

Anne chose what would end up being a small statue of Mary wearing a veil and halo. I chose what would be a statue of Joseph.

"Now that your plaster is stirred and thick, scoop some out with your spoon and pour it into the mold." Pamela demonstrated the procedure with a mold of a little church. Anne tipped her spoon filled with plaster into the bottom of her Mary mold. I did the same with my Joseph mold. Once they were filled to the top, Pamela told us to put the molds on the metal rack she had prepared on the shelf beside our worktable. Then we ran outside to play volleyball.

The next morning, Pamela showed us how to peel the rubber mold away from the solid, hard plaster. The statues emerged. My Joseph was squished in the middle, and his head looked deformed. Air bubbles had become trapped inside the plaster before it had set, ruining my Joseph. But Anne's statue of Mary was perfect. Pamela produced ten small paint boxes and paintbrushes, and we proceeded to paint the statues. I painted St. Joseph's robe purple, his beard black, and his hair brown. By the time I was finished, he looked like a clown. Anne gave her Mary a blue veil, yellow hair, and a light-blue robe.

As Anne and I walked home that summer afternoon, I pulled my crummy statue out of my pocket and smashed it against a wall. Anne ran ahead of me, and I never caught up.

By the time I walked into the house, my mother was already praising Anne's pretty little statue. I liked it too. "Anne, this is such a beautiful gift," my mother told her. "And I like the pretty colors too." They hugged, and then my mother looked at me from across the kitchen, smiled, and blew me a kiss. My mother said, "I know just where I will put this little statue of Mary." She stood up, reached across the sink, and placed Mary on the shelf at the base of the window.

Forty years later, that plaster-of-paris statue of Mary still sits on the same shelf. My parents have been married for fifty-five years, and they still live in the house that they bought in 1948. We have a hard time imagining the future of our world. But it seems that we can imagine what heaven will be like. It will be like a woman smiling and hugging her children.

The Fog Comes on Little Cat Feet

My sister Anne unwittingly set me on the path to heaven. When she was a little girl, she knew how to braid daisies into a crown, where the best cherry tree was, and when the fruit was good for picking. It was Anne who taught me to savor the taste of green peppers and how to inhale the scent of honeysuckle.

One afternoon, as I was lying on the living-room floor and coloring, Anne entered the room and recited over and over again, "The fog comes on little cat feet. The fog comes on little cat feet." I did not know that these were the first words of Carl Sandburg's famous little poem "Fog." To this day, I do not know where Anne heard the poem or why she memorized the words, but I remember how she pranced around the living room with her arms above her head as she recited the line.

At the time, I did not understand the metaphor. I did not see the connection between the low, creeping fog and a low, creeping cat. But I heard something. I turned my head in Anne's direction as she repeated these words, because I liked how they fit together and how they sounded like music. So I began to chant the words as well: "Fog comes on little cat feet."

If we want to find our way to heaven, we have to come to the realization that there is a place beyond our immediate selves. Michael tried to stretch way beyond Australia in his imagination in order to visualize a place where God is waiting for us. However we define that place, it ends up being the center of our lives as Christians. That small bit of poetry my sister chanted helped me recognize there was something significant about the words, but I could not exactly explain what. I began my quest for an explanation for something significant that I could not exactly explain, but I knew it was there. Poetry has helped me, all of my life, to imagine a center within myself that seems to respond to beauty and goodness in a way that pulls me toward something beyond the routines of a regular day.

We like music and poetry and certain paintings in the museum in the same way that birds know how to fly. It is in our nature to do so. It is our nature to love what is beautiful, and in such beauty there are hints of the first beauty, which is God. We love Mozart because he taps into the first beauty. He hints at the center.

We make mistakes about what is at the center. We sometimes think that we are the center of the universe. Our ancestors thought that the sun was the center. Now we think that the center of all things can be found in the genome embedded deep inside the DNA strand. The center determines the shape of our lives. Place money in the center and we are defined by big bank accounts, big cars, and fancy vacations. Place self at the center and we become arrogant with plaques of achievement, college degrees, and loneliness hanging on our walls. But if we place God at the center, what emanates? I think it is that feeling of undisturbed, unrestrained love that we can sometimes sense when we listen to the heart within. We are not God, nor are we gods. But we have come from God. In a sense we are the light emanating from the heart of God. Listening to my sister recite poetry in my adult memory is like listening to Mozart. I touch that simpler original beauty. We are not God. We live with God inside of us.

We are in the habit of turning our heads toward things that attract us. We hear something to our right—a horn, a bird, someone laughing—and we turn our heads in the direction of the sudden sound. Whenever I see a blimp, I turn my head upward with wonder and point to anyone near. "Look at the size of that thing." It is the same with our center-self, our God-self. How do we come to such knowledge? And who is this inside person, and where is she or he going? I know I have to make the trip to the store this afternoon, and I know I will walk under the maple trees in the neighborhood, then down the road past the Smiths' house, and then I will take a right and enter the small village and complete my trip. I will reach into the tall refrigerator of the store and wrap my fingers around the top of the cool bottle of milk. The soul's journey is not so exact, but it ought to be. The soul's destination isn't as easy to define, but it ought to be. There is a thin border between the physical self and the spiritual self. We have to first introduce one to the other deep within ourselves, and before that, we have to acknowledge the existence of both before any formal introduction can take place. It is, perhaps, our goal in life to introduce ourselves to God and to form a lasting relationship.

A baby does not *know* it has a spiritual dimension. Most children do not *know* this. Slowly, slowly, we come to a dream beyond logic, to a fantasy beyond reason that allows us to recognize this spiritual self. We first come to this knowledge by a sudden turn of the head toward a sound, by a sudden prick in the eternal part of ourselves. I think it is God's voice in us.

I began my journey to the center of myself when I heard my sister repeating the words of Carl Sandburg. I didn't know this then, of course, but now that I take a backward glance, I can see how such a small event began my journey toward becoming a writer, which is really my way of communicating with my spiritual self.

I believe we all seek our true center, and if we find it, we find God.

V

SUFFERING

California Girl

The path to heaven is filled with suffering. None of us can escape it. Sometimes suffering seems to enclose us in a prison of misery. My mother endured a painful recovery from cancer surgery. A neighbor suddenly died last Thursday. Another neighbor lost his job. A friend wrote a letter saying that after fifteen years of marriage, his wife had filed for a divorce. Christ suffers with us. He suffered and died and rose from the dead to free us from the prison of suffering. In him we have hope. We are all like the biblical Job who endured a great loss, but are we all like Job who stayed faithful to God despite all that was lost?

I started to think of this question during my first week of college, when I met someone whose suffering was greater than any suffering I had known.

I met her soon after I arrived at the university, in September of 1969. I had stepped into a seafood restaurant for dinner. The restaurant was really a bar with a small dining section. I sat in the dining section, and while I was trying to decide if I would spend the money and get the shrimp, I noticed a girl sitting at the bar having a loud conversation with the bartender. I could not help but overhear the conversation. The girl was talking about California, about the ocean and how much she loved the sun. The bartender didn't believe she was from California because she didn't have a tan and she wasn't blond. The girl started to get angry and pulled out her driver's license. "And I have a picture of myself with my Goddamn mother and my Goddamn father." She handed him the picture. "That's me in the middle." She told the bartender that everyone in California has babies and sends them to school and to Scouts or softball teams or playgroups, and by the time the babies are ready for college, they don't care about the sun any longer, or the ocean.

I ordered the shrimp and ate my dinner slowly. As I was finishing up, the girl at the bar was given her tab: twenty-nine dollars. "I don't have twenty-nine dollars," she said, and the bartender asked, "Well, how much do you have?" and the girl said five dollars. "Well, that's not enough," he answered; then the girl reached down into her blouse, wiggled a bit, pulled out her bra, and handed it to the man. "Paid in full," she said, and then she walked out the door.

I paid for my meal and then walked outside, where I found the girl on the ground next to the building, her face buried in her arms. She was curled into a ball, like a discarded seashell on the hard beach of the cement sidewalk. I stepped up to her, leaned over, and asked if she was all right. She looked up at me and asked, "Do you know Degas?" I helped her stand up and asked her where she lived, and she said she lived at the university. When I told her that I did too, she said, "Show me your damn license to prove it." Then she began to stagger. "Degas," she said, "he knew women." I asked the girl her name, and that is how I first met Cherylann.

We were walking back toward campus when she thought she heard a distant train whistle. "Hey," she said. "There are trains around here? I grew up next to trains. Let's find the trains." I tried to dissuade her as she stumbled down the sidewalk. I tried to lead her back to the dorm, but she would have none of it. "I want to go catch a damn train."

We found the train tracks beside the river. Cherylann dropped to her knees and put her ear on the track. "I can't hear anything," she said, and then she made me put my ear on the track. But all I could hear was her crying. I helped her stand up, and she started talking about Degas again, how he observed women when they weren't looking and got inside of them with his brush and paint and color and passion. She used that word, *passion,* a great deal, and then she made me laugh. She started talking about Popeye. "You know, I like that show. I like it when he opens up that can of spinach and becomes strong. His whole body bulges out. I saw one cartoon where Brutus was running away with Olive Oyl. He had her locked in the caboose, and Brutus was the engineer bearing down on Popeye, who was tied to the tracks up ahead." Cherylann told me that Popeye saw the train coming and used his pipe as a blowtorch to open the can of spinach that was sticking out of his pocket, and then he used the pipe to suck the spinach into his mouth. "Popeye's muscles began to bulge, and the ropes snapped off, and Popeye stood on those tracks, raised up his two hands, made two fists, and clubbed the train to a stop. How come we can't do that?" Cherylann asked me. "How come we can't eat something that will make us strong and catch trains like Popeye?"

Cherylann asked me if I would catch a train with her. I knew she was drunk and that I couldn't leave her alone, but I also knew that a train was on its way, because we both heard the whistle in the distance. "Don't worry," she said. "We'll do it like this. We'll stand as close as we can. We'll be Popeye as much as we can. My father filled me with enough damn spinach to make me bulge." Then Cherylann threw up, right there on the tracks. The train was coming, and she stood up and placed the tips of her shoes against the outside rail. Then she took two steps backward and asked me to stand beside her. "My father," Cherylann said, "was like a train when he came down those tracks when I turned seventeen, and he saw inside of me and I couldn't stop him with my raised fists and spinach." She held my hand as the train rushed by us with one loud and long blast of the horn.

I brought Cherylann back to the dorm and helped her get settled in her bed. Then I walked down the hall, stepped outside, and heard, again, a distant train whistle.

The next morning, Cherylann knocked on my door and handed me a letter as she entered my room. "I'm sorry about last night," Cherylann said. "My brother . . . I just found out he was killed in Vietnam. I'm going home this afternoon. Thanks for saving my life. I've never been drunk before."

Cherylann asked me to read the letter. I took it in my hand, slowly tore open the envelope, and then read the letter while Cherylann leaned back against the wall, closing her eyes, letting the shadows of the room cover her face.

Dear Cherylann:

By the time you receive this letter, we'll be miles from here. We are always moving. I'm sorry that I won't be home for Christmas. Can you imagine that? I'm twenty-four years old and this is the first time I'll be away for the holidays. We're planning our own Christmas party, though I don't think I should go into too many details. You wouldn't approve.

We're all a bit on edge. Maybe because of the upcoming holiday. I wish sometimes that I would hear a good reason why we're here. We're told that the people here want their freedom from the north and China, and that they want democracy, but it seems to me that most of the people I met over here want food. I guess we just follow orders. People in Washington probably know what they are doing. You just have to believe in authority in this man's army. I wonder, though, if they ever think that they made a mistake and they just don't know how to get out of it. I do know this:

there are many people in power who are doing everything they can to keep that power. Why is it that we have to live under someone's thumb? There seems to always be someone above us who thinks he is better or smarter or wiser, who has to keep some great mystery that must be protected from us poor, ignorant soldiers. I don't have anywhere to go except across the next field because that is where I was told to go. When I get out of here, I'm going to find a job where I can be pretty much left alone. Remember how Dad hated his job, always saying that he felt trapped working for people he didn't respect, following rules that he didn't have any say in. I don't want to live like that.

I hope everything is okay with you at school. I read the college scores and I think it's great that your basketball team is clobbering everyone. Your school has a good chance at winning the whole NCAA championship.

The kids here play a type of soccer with a pigskin ball. It's real pigskin. You can see the bristles on a new ball that a kid just made. They play in the rain. You should see these kids run.

Say hi to mom. I think she's going to marry that guy she met at work. It's strange seeing mom with someone else, but if she's happy, I guess that's what counts. I'd better go.

I'll see you in the spring.

Love ya,

Billy

When Cherylann returned to campus after her brother's funeral, she said, "At my brother's funeral, they gave my mother a medal, and an officer shook her hand. He shook my hand too. He wore these pure-white gloves. I wanted to peel off the gloves and hold the man's bare hands. It's important to me, nothing being covered.

"Do you know that at the grave in the cemetery they cover the dirt with a layer of fake grass? Apparently we're not supposed to see the dirt that will be dumped into the hole. They do it with a backhoe, but we're not supposed to see that either. It was strange, after the priest spoke and the officers spoke and someone played taps, we all got up and walked away, leaving the coffin above the grave. I wanted to stay and watch the coffin being lowered into the ground. I wanted to see the dirt fill up the hole. I just didn't want to leave like that."

Cherlyann endured the abuse of her father and the death of her brother. She and I were friends for the rest of our college days together. After college, she got married, became a teacher and a mother. The last I heard from her was in a small note:

> . . . I came across your books and thought I would write. . . . I haven't seen my father in thirty years. He has three grandchildren: all girls. I forgave him in my heart many years ago. I know where he lives, and I sent him a picture of my daughters. I just want him to know that I forgive him. I hope he makes it to heaven someday. In heaven he will understand Degas and trains, and he will understand and love me.

In Luke 7:22, it is written, "The blind receive sight, the lame walk, those who have leprosy are cured, the deaf hear, the dead are raised, and the good news is preached to the poor."

Heaven is a place where the blind see, the sick are cured, the deaf hear, and the dead are raised, all because of God's love. Heaven is a place where we understand the beauty of Degas, where we dance with a brother who died in Vietnam, and where we forgive those who trespassed against us.

Hugs and Curses

I was walking in midtown Manhattan recently, on my way home from a meeting with some editors and writers, when I was suddenly approached by five children, about nine or ten years old. "Mister," one of the children said to me, "what's your name?"

I didn't answer.

"Mister. What's your name?" he asked again. Then I noticed that the other children were surrounding me. I felt little hands groping in my jacket and back pockets. I reached behind me and grabbed a small hand that was closing around my wallet.

"Mister, you got a name?"

I brushed the hands away. "What are you doing?" I asked in fear.

Instead of answering, one of the children spit in my face. Then he and the others quickly ran down the street and disappeared.

When children are led to believe that the world is not a joyous place, but a brutal place, their lives become precarious. As I wiped my brow, I was reminded of the time I first learned this lesson.

I was a freshman in college, and I had read in the school newspaper that the local orphanage was accepting student volunteers to help out on weekends. With four friends, I decided to volunteer.

The orphanage, which was five miles from the university, was set back from the main highway and surrounded by rough lawns, oak trees, and a driveway of crushed stones. We drove up to the main building, where we were greeted by a woman who told us that the children had just finished lunch and were playing out back. She invited us to join them and introduce ourselves.

My friends and I walked along the crushed stones, past a barn, and around the corner of the main house. Then we stopped. At least thirty children, ranging in age from two to thirteen, were running, shouting, jumping rope, and laughing, until, one by one, they saw us standing in the shadows and grew quiet.

A few of the older children stepped toward us, and the younger children followed. A girl about eleven or twelve reached her hand toward me and asked, "What's your name?"

"Chris," I answered as we shook hands.

"I'm Brenda. My parents are dead."

Gradually our novelty wore off, and the children began to play again, their shouting and laughing once more filling the courtyard. For the first half-hour, we college students played catch, Mother May I?, and leapfrog. The more comfortable the children felt around us, the more affectionate they became. They jumped on us and insisted that we give them piggyback rides. They tickled us. We played a game similar to musical chairs and ring-around-the-rosy, and at the end of the game, Brenda and I were the last ones in the middle of the circle. She turned to me and gave me one of the most loving embraces I've ever felt. Then all the children piled on top of us. Brenda's black, curly hair was covered with oak leaves. We all laughed and laughed until a harsh buzzer emanated from a loudspeaker attached to one of the trees.

The children stood up immediately and started walking back to the main house in silence. The woman who had greeted us at the main entrance held the door open for the children. Then she walked over to the five of us as we were brushing the dirt and leaves from our hair and clothes. With little grace, she said to us, "We don't allow the children to touch the guests. They will get too attached. You don't have to come here again."

She turned and walked away. We were never invited back to the orphanage. I never saw Brenda again.

Like the children I encountered in the city that day, the orphans I befriended that afternoon years ago had been deprived of something essential—the ability to love and accept love. We need to show children how to love and be loved, and thus set them on the path to heaven. My heart aches for these children who spit in our faces and aren't allowed to experience a loving embrace. It is difficult not to feel hopeless about such situations, not to overlook the damage being caused to these children. But then I remember that God wants to heal our damaged spirits and that Jesus is our eternal hope, and I get a glimpse of heaven. With faith, we can create a world in which every child is invited into a loving embrace.

The Power of the Powerless

The plot of the famous film *Miracle on 34th Street* revolved around the claim that an old man named Chris was, in reality, Kris Kringle. During the trial scene, the Unites States Post Office delivered to the courthouse thousands of letters children had written to Santa Claus. The defense attorney offered this as proof that this old man was the real St. Nicholas. After all, the attorney stated, if the Unites States government proclaimed that this man was Santa Claus, who were we to doubt such authority?

What if we read about heaven in the *Wall Street Journal*? Do we have a higher authority in our secular world beyond the *Wall Street Journal*. Actually, this happened once. When I give talks, I often make a reference to a particular line that was published in one of my most widely read essays that the *Journal* published in 1985: "When I was small my mother would say, 'Isn't it wonderful that you can see?' And once she said, 'When you go to heaven, Oliver will run to you, embrace you, and the first thing he will say is 'Thank you.'"

I stand at the podium and read those lines and I stop, hold up the essay and say to the audience, "See? Right here: 'When you go to heaven . . .' In the *Wall Street Journal*." The people sitting in their seats ponder the juxtaposition: The *Wall Street Journal* and heaven; the secular world and the spiritual world. Of course, the *Wall Street Journal* doesn't endorse the existence of heaven because they printed a few words about a mother speaking about such a place. But still, hints of a spiritual reality crop up sometimes in the most unlikely places.

My brother Oliver was more than a hint of spiritual reality. He was the whole package. I believe that Oliver was a messenger from God. Oliver could not see, think, speak, or hold a fork or glass. All Oliver needed in order to survive was for someone to love him. That is all Christ asked us to do for each other. Oliver survived for thirty-two years because others fed and bathed him, kept him warm with blankets, and loved him. "What you do for the least of my brothers, you do for me." We can read about heaven in the Bible. We can listen to our mothers explain heaven's existence. And, on this occasion, flip through the newspapers and find a young man feeding his brother as his future bride watches, and sees, and loves.

• • •

THE POWER OF THE POWERLESS

I grew up in the house where my brother was on his back in his bed for almost thirty-three years, in the same corner of his room, under the same window; beside the same yellow walls. Oliver was blind, mute. His legs were twisted. He didn't have the strength to lift his head nor the intelligence to learn anything.

Today I am an English teacher, and each time I intro-duce my class to the play about Helen Keller, The Miracle Worker, *I tell my students about Oliver. One day, during my first year teaching, a boy in the last row raised his hand and said, "Oh, Mr. de Vinck. You mean he was a vegetable."*

I stammered for a few seconds. My family and I fed Oliver. We changed his diapers, hung his clothes and bed linen on the basement line in winter, and spread them out white and clean on the lawn in the summer. I always liked to watch the grasshoppers jump on the pillowcases.

We bathed Oliver. Tickled his chest to make him laugh. Sometimes we left the radio on in his room. We pulled the shade down over his bed in the morning to keep the sun from burning his tender skin. We listened to him laugh as we watched television downstairs. We listened to him rock his arms up and down to make the bed squeak. We listened to him cough in the middle of the night.

"Well, I guess you could call him a vegetable. I called him Oliver, my brother. You would have liked him."

One October day in 1946, when my mother was pregnant with Oliver, her second son, she was overcome by fumes from a leaking coal-burning stove. My oldest brother was sleeping in his crib, which was quite high off the ground so the gas didn't affect him. My father pulled them outside, where my mother revived quickly.

On April 20, 1947, Oliver was born, a healthy looking, plump, beautiful boy. One afternoon, a few months later, my mother brought Oliver to a window. She held him there in the sun, the bright good sun, and there Oliver looked and looked directly into the sunlight, which was the first moment my mother realized that Oliver was blind. My parents, the true heroes of this story, learned with the passing months that blindness was only part of the problem. So they brought Oliver to Mt. Sinai Hospital in New York for tests to determine the extent of his condition.

The doctor said that he wanted to make it very clear to both my mother and father that there was absolutely nothing that could be done for Oliver. He didn't want my parents to grasp at false hope. "You could place him in an institution," he said. "But," my parents answered, "he is our son. We will take Oliver home of course." The good doctor answered, "Then take him home and love him."

Oliver grew to the size of a ten year old. He had a big chest, a large head. His hands and feet were those of a five year old: small and soft. We'd wrap a box of baby cereal for him at Christmas and place it under the tree; pat his head with a damp cloth in the middle of a July heat wave. His baptismal certificate hung on the wall above his head. A bishop came to the house and confirmed him.

Even now, twenty-one years after his death from pneumonia on March 12, 1980, Oliver still remains the weakest, most helpless human being I ever met, and yet he was one of the most powerful human beings I ever met. He could do absolutely nothing except breathe, sleep, eat, and yet he was responsible for action, love, courage, insight. When I was small my mother would say, "Isn't it wonderful that you can see?" And once she said, "When you go to heaven, Oliver will run to you, embrace you, and the first thing he will say is 'Thank you.'" I remember, too, my mother explaining to me that we were blessed with Oliver in ways that were not clear to her at first.

So often parents are faced with a child who is severely retarded, but who is also hyperactive, demanding, or wild, who needs constant care. So many people have little choice but to place their child in an institution. We were fortunate that Oliver didn't need us to be in his room all day. He never knew what his condition was. We were blessed with his presence, a true presence of peace.

When I was in my early twenties, I met a girl and fell in love. After a few months I brought her home to meet my family. When my mother went to the kitchen to prepare dinner, I asked the girl, "Would you like to see Oliver?" for I had told her about my brother. "No," she answered.

Soon after, I met Roe, a lovely girl. She asked me the names of my brothers and sisters. She loved children. I thought she was wonderful. I brought her home after a few months to meet my family. Soon it was time for me to feed

Oliver. I remember sheepishly asking Roe if she'd like to see him. "Sure," she said.

I sat at Oliver's bedside as Roe watched over my shoulder. I gave him his first spoonful. His second. "Can I do that?" Roe asked with ease, with freedom, with compassion, so I gave her the bowl and she fed Oliver one spoonful at a time.

The power of the powerless. Which girl would you marry? Today Roe and I have three children.

How to Increase the Total Amount of Happiness

Peter Singer, the controversial Australian bioethicist, holds the prestigious Ira W. DeCamp Professorship of Bioethics at Princeton University's Center for Human Values. Not surprisingly, advocates for the disabled vigorously protested his selection. Professor Singer is an outspoken advocate for euthanasia not only for terminally ill adults, but also for severely disabled infants. He wrote in his influential textbook *Practical Ethics* that "killing a disabled infant is not morally equivalent to killing a person. Very often it is not wrong at all." Why? If the parents kill this disabled child and have a child they would not otherwise have, Singer argues, "the loss of a happy life for the first infant is outweighed by the gain of a happier life for the second," thus increasing "the total amount of happiness."

When I read this, I wondered what Professor Singer's reaction would have been had he met my mother Catherine and my brother Oliver. I wonder how Professor Singer would react to my *Wall Street Journal* essay about Oliver. I sent him the article and my book of the same title, but, not surprisingly, I never received an answer from him. How is it that one person, my wife for instance, can ask to help feed Oliver, and another person, Professor Singer for instance, is comfortable with killing him?

Tending to Oliver's needs was part of the normal routine my mother and father created for our family. For example, it was a normal thing to make sure that Oliver had a cold drink of water two or three times a day during an August heat wave. When I was very young I thought that everyone had a brother like Oliver. He was not the center of the family. Oliver was simply part of the family, just like everyone else. My sister Anne and I often carried Oliver down the hall for a warm bath. At his bedside, she would place her hands under his knees and I would place my hands under his arms, and together we would lift Oliver as my mother called out instructions. "Lift him slowly. Don't back up into the chair, Chris. Watch his elbows. Don't bump his elbows against the door frame." This was ordinary family life.

During his thirty-two years of life, Oliver brought surprising gifts into my mother's life, but she admitted this was not apparent to her at first. When he was born, my mother initially wept, hid her tears and grief and sadness from her family. Yet because of Oliver, my mother began asking bigger questions: Why these circumstances of life? Why her family? What is the meaning of its mystery? How do we live with the knowledge of what could have been in the face of what is? Most of us will know this sort of pain at one time or another in our lives. But not all of us have the courage to stick with someone like Oliver, loving him in the face of all the impossible hurdles.

Professor Singer, no doubt, would have counseled my mother to place him in an institution, free herself of this "burden," thus increasing the "total amount of happiness." But how does one measure the worth of Oliver's laugh, the color of his eyes, the feel of his tender skin, and the influence Oliver would make on a world obsessed with power and comfort and physical perfection?

I wrote an article about Oliver for the *Wall Street Journal*. Hundreds of people wrote me letters about the powerless people in their lives. Eunice Kennedy Shriver and her husband, Sargent Shriver, invited me to Washington, D.C., to write for the Special Olympics. President Reagan read the article in the White House that morning and sent me a personal letter in celebration of Oliver's existence. The pope invited me to the Vatican to deliver the closing speech at an international conference on disabilities. I was asked to end the conference with the story of Oliver, and then I, Oliver's brother, was brought to meet the pope. The *Reader's Digest,* the Chicago papers, the New York papers, and dozens of other newspapers and magazines reprinted my essay. The little article grew into *The Power of the Powerless,* the first of my ten books.

All this came from the small seed of Oliver's helplessness. He set into motion the parable of his life, which influenced millions of people around the world. People recognized the strength Oliver possessed. We are all weak. We all need help. Oliver survived because for thirty-two years other human beings placed food at his lips, and with each meal, Oliver was nourished. With each meal we who gave him food and drink were nourished. Oliver survived on compassion. We all survive on compassion.

In accepting Oliver for who he was rather than lamenting what he was not, my mother rose to a new level of understanding that enriched her in the same way that many people are enriched by tending to those they love. Pearl Buck, the Nobel Prize winner, wrote about her severely disabled daughter in her slim classic *The Child Who Never Grew*: "There must be acceptance and the knowledge that sorrow fully accepted brings its own gifts. For there is an alchemy in sorrow. It can be transmuted into wisdom, which, if it does not bring joy, can yet being happiness."

Sorrow pricks our hearts and, like any wound, causes pain. We seek solace from the hurt, and in the hunt for solace we find God, or husband, or wife, or friend, or self in the most significant levels of meaning. In the hunt for solace we discover who we are, and such a discovery can lead us to the revelation of inner peace. I do not know why this is so, but it is. If we do not look for the joy in the sorrow, the sorrow will consume us, and we will perish.

Over the long distance between Oliver's birth and his death, my mother believed there was a unity of purpose in the journey, a sense that all will be well on this earth. This assurance sustained and strengthened my mother and confirmed her faith, which ultimately brought happiness.

She believed in what might be called the power of the powerless, the mystery of sadness, and in the lost chances that paradoxically opened her to other possibilities. Because she was confined to the house, my mother fed her tested soul with books, prayer, longing, the laughter of her other children, and the grace of a merciful God. Because my mother said yes to life, she decided to have four more children and to pass along to each of us a vision that the Peter Singers of the world might never understand.

When my father was asked how he managed to tend to Oliver's needs for thirty-two years, he just said, "It was not thirty-two years. It was one day at a time. Can I feed Oliver today? Yes. Can I bathe Oliver today? Yes. Can I love Oliver today? Yes."

When we are confronted with emotional pain, or loss, or sadness, what do we do? Some of us give up. Some destroy all that is around us. Some push away everything that is good. Some of us encase hope in a box and carry it up to the attic, never to open it again. And then there are other people who embrace their sadness and the possibility of peace, no matter how impossible or distant it seems to be.

Can we be sad one day at a time? Can we love one day at a time? Can we handle our great joy one day at a time? Can we tend to our inner turmoil one day at a time? Yes we can. And will all this lead to peace? Yes, yes it will, if we tend to the burdens of our lives with love, faith, hope, charity, joy, courage, dignity, humor. My mother's faithfulness taught me this. Oliver taught me this.

Academic truth based on dry, unfeeling logic would never have quenched Oliver's thirst in an August heat wave. Fortunately, we are far better people than the bioethicists could ever imagine.

It is too bad that Peter Singer never carried my brother Oliver down the hall to the warm bathtub. That hallway is a small passage to heaven.

Fix My Mother

Last week my mother was diagnosed with lung cancer. At the beginning of the month, she had spit up a bit of blood, spurring her to make an appointment with an ear, throat, and nose specialist. The doctor said that he believed the blood was due to an irritation in her throat, perhaps from burst blood vessels, but he asked her to go for a chest X-ray just in case.

A week later, my mother sat before her regular doctor and an oncologist, both of whom looked glum as they explained to her that on her left lung was a tumor the size of a golf ball.

Last week my mother had a CAT scan and a complete bone scan of her body to make sure that the cancer hadn't spread. Next week she'll go to Memorial Sloan-Kettering Cancer Center in New York City, where the doctors will determine the type of cancer she has, the surgery that will be needed, and the follow-up care she will have to undergo.

My mother said to me, "I am not going to die yet, Christopher. And I am not afraid. I have been a prayerful person all my life. I am seventy-eight years old. Do you think that I will abandon hope, prayer, and God now, simply because I am ill?"

"You seem more worried about the cat being lost than you are about this tumor," I said.

"But, Christopher, I worry a great deal about the cat. It has been missing for two days, but this tumor, this suffering, will bring me grace, and grace comes from God, so it would be foolish to worry about the cancer. What brings us grace should be celebrated. If we trust in God, we cannot worry. I do not receive any grace because the cat is lost in the woods, so I worry about the cat."

Do I shake my fists at God and warn him, "Fix my mother!" Despite what my mother says, I cannot express gratitude to God for my mother's illness. I cannot sing. This was not in my plan. This is not what I imagined for my life. I want to keep things just as they are. I want God to fix things so that they remain the same.

I have a habit of dreaming. This doesn't seem to be a time to take refuge in dreams, but perhaps this is a good time to do that. I easily fall into the intoxication of a dreamworld. When I am lonely, or worried about one of my children, I daydream about "the way things used to be." Sometimes I imagine that I am speaking with my grandmother, or that I am climbing trees with my little sister. Sometimes I imagine that I am speaking with God. I sometimes imagine that God speaks in the voice of my mother, or in the sound from a bassoon. I hope God's voice sounds like my daughter giggling, or like Mr. Jones who owns the hardware store. Mr. Jones likes to tease his customers, and he knows all there is to know about paint and hinges. I like that image of God: a great tease who knows where everything is in his store.

Or I remember the late great dreamer Henri Nouwen. Henri was nostalgic for heaven. He always imagined what life could be like if we all lived with the joyous recognition that both God and heaven are real. When Henri invited me to Harvard for a few days, he and I prayed first thing in the morning. We prayed at breakfast and after breakfast. As we walked to his morning class, he told me a sad story about his pet goat. When he was a boy he owned a goat, and during the war, someone ate the goat. I do not remember much of the story, except that he was horrified.

As we entered an academic building, many students called out, "Good morning, Henri." Inside the classroom perhaps 150 students were sitting in their seats. Henri took off his hat and coat, opened a binder with disheveled papers, and indicated to a student that he was ready. The student stood up and led the class in a Taizé chant, the Jubilate Deo, and the young people sang and sang in prayer. At the end, Henri began his lecture—Henri Nouwen, theologian and goat lover.

I would like to capture Henri's joyous spirit now. My problem is that I do not know how to deal with a world that is not joyous. All I see around me is the power of decay. I see it in the wilting spring flowers and in the eyes of my troubled high school students. I see it in the sickness of my mother. How do we live joyously with the knowledge that the dream we once had is broken?

This feeling of sadness for my mother is new. I have felt it only once before, when as a child I realized that someday my mother and father were going to die. But I quickly put the notion aside, as children do, and learned not to believe in death any more than I believed in Santa Claus. And now here I am, fifty years old, and I must revisit the possibility of my mother's dying. I cry and weep. My rational self battles my spiritual self. Now is the time to believe not just in the dream of God and the dream of heaven. Now is the time to believe in the reality of God and the reality of heaven.

I always believed in heaven, but never as an immediate reality. Now I must learn how to believe in heaven as a reality, because my mother might die. Yes, my mother is going to die. Not today, not this week, not even this year. But she will die someday. It took me fifty years to believe this. And it all happened so suddenly. *Boom.* Your mother has cancer. *Poof.* Life is no longer as it was. Do you believe in God and heaven and grace?

The morning after my mother told me the news, I woke up in my bed to find the room cold. Roe had left the window open, and a cold autumn air had filled the room with its night breathing. The tigers of my dreams melted into the towels that hung on the rack by the door.

As I took my shower that morning, after my mother told me she had cancer, I watched the water disappear into the drain at my feet. I just wanted to run back into my mother's arms, but the water kept turning and turning, disappearing down the drain. We endure little deaths along the way of our lives. We cannot return to the old neighborhood. Mothers die, but I believe there is an old man in Australia who can send a message back.

VI
HOME

My Earthly Mansion

Speaking to his disciples about heaven, Jesus said, "In my father's house there are many mansions." I like to think that our homes give us a hint of heaven. But in my case, it's more than a hint. When Roe and I first stepped into the house that we've been living in for the past twenty-four years, I was sure we were embarking on a spiritual adventure.

In the fall of 1977, I left my father's house and began my new life with Roe in a two-story, four-bedroom American colonial house that we had purchased from an older couple. Roe and I were immediately drawn to the yard, just a small plot of land, yet home to ten large oak trees, each about five or six stories tall. The previous owners had surrounded the base of each tree with periwinkle. A dignified concrete birdbath stood in the middle of the yard, its open bowl generously inviting one and all.

Since I've lived in this house, I've planted grass seed twenty-four times, fertilized intermittently, attacked grubs, built a shed, erected two swing sets, and assembled one sandbox. Ten years after we moved in, Roe and I hired a builder to construct an addition to the house. Five years later we hired someone else to assemble a deck. With each new construction, we cut into our small tract of land.

A small, sturdy clay pot sits in the southwestern corner of the yard. When our first son, David, was four years old, I carried that pot from the garage, turned it upside down, and placed it in the corner under the mock-orange bush. I called this a secret place, and for years David liked to run to that small seat and hide under the bush. The pot is still there. Today David is twenty-two.

The birdbath is gone. It cracked one winter, and Roe and I placed the base and broken bowl on the curb for the trash collection.

The children have trampled all the periwinkle into dust during their games of running bases or Mother May I? or baseball.

I've buried six goldfish, four mice, a chipmunk, and a robin under the rhododendron. In the backyard, the children have slept in the tent, played catch, and conquered territory with their water balloons. They have eaten hamburgers and watermelons during summer barbecues and dodged each other's snowballs in the winter.

One year Roe and I planted raspberries in the north-western portion of the yard. In late October that year, I was delighted to find a single raspberry—a last piece of summer to be savored in October. I picked the bit of fruit and pressed it between my tongue and the roof of my mouth. Later, the raspberries began to encroach on the neighbor's property and, it seemed, on everything else, so I pulled up the plants and dragged them to the town compost dump.

The swing sets are gone. The sandbox is gone. Even the children are almost gone. David is twenty-two and a graduate student. Karen is nineteen. Michael is seventeen. Our dog is eight years old.

It is nighttime, mid-January, as I write. For some reason, the temperature jumped to fifty-five degrees today. The floodlight is on. I look out my window and see a single moth dancing in the light. Old, dirty snow covers the backyard. I like the backyard better in summer. Sometimes I walk out into the yard when the moon is full, sit on the grass, and look up at the moon shining through the leaves of an oak tree. I just sit and look. Sometimes I pat the ground and our dog emerges from the darkness to sit beside me. Sometimes

I take off my shoes and socks. I pat the dirt. I linger in finite time with my growing children. I find my way back to that day when Roe and I bought our little house and land, when the days were young and the moon spoke out with optimism and hope.

Someday Roe and I will drive the car out to the garden center, pick up some periwinkle, drive home, and surround each tree in the lawn with the plant. We'll buy another cement birdbath, and then we'll hammer a For Sale sign into the generous earth of the front lawn. Perhaps Roe will have to put that sign up by herself; perhaps I will have to do it alone. We cannot know the day of our own death, but we can measure the distance we have come since the day we first stepped into this house.

This house is my earthly mansion. It is here where I spent most of my time. It is here where our children were conceived. It is here where I wrote all of my books. It is here where I picked daffodils each spring. And it is here where my physical world will probably end someday. Then I'll go to a heavenly mansion. But the present mansion is connected to the future one. It is a good place. I think it is a lot like heaven.

Bees in the Attic

Now that I am fifty, an old struggle in my heart takes on a new character. Some illusions are gone. I no longer believe that national and international affairs are seen clearly in my daily copy of the *New York Times*. Ambition and fame are no longer gilded in my mind. I sometimes have my bouts of loneliness. I sometimes feel more lost and more alone than I will ever understand. I sometimes think that I have already seen the best part of my life, and I carry this part of me, this winter, into the night when I go to sleep.

Yet I am more certain of my faith than I have ever been before. Roe and our children surround me. I have a number of loyal friends, and I am grateful for their love. I work in a large school district where I feel I am making a difference. I feel as if I am a part of the broader community as a student, a teacher, a father, and a writer. I still like to taste snow, and I am not afraid of growing old.

And yet, I have hope in the notion that this life I have created, with its disappointments and imperfections, will one day be reconstructed. Perhaps that notion is another hint of heaven.

Two weeks ago, Roe called down to me from the attic, where she had been searching for Christmas decorations. "Chris, you'd better come up here and take a look at this." I climbed the narrow wooden steps into the attic, where Roe was pointing through the dim light to the far wall. There, attached to the wall, was a beehive the size of a stuffed pillow. I began to crawl toward the gray mass. Then I realized that if I disturbed the nest and the bees swarmed at me, I would not be able to make a hasty retreat, so I backed away. If the hive had been on the outside of the house, attached to the gutter or the chimney, I would have simply knocked it down and sent the bees on their way. But here in the house, with hundreds, perhaps thousands, of bees sluggishly waiting in their hive for spring, direct action was too risky. I decided to call an exterminator.

After I made the call, I climbed the steps into the attic once again, peered through the dim light at the beehive, and whispered, "Fly away. Fly away. They are coming to get you." Then I walked back down the stairs into the house and pushed the narrow steps up into the ceiling.

I don't like to kill things, especially bees. I identify with bees. They fly, walk, produce, dance, all for the purpose of procreation and the development of a food source. They are heavy in their tasks as they move back and forth from home to flower and back again. They tend to the queen, build hives, and generally carry out the script of their existence. I, of course, do these things too.

The exterminator arrived at the house at exactly 4:00 the next day. He told me that he was going to inject a powder into the hive, wait a few minutes for the bees to die, and then break up the nest.

I heard the man clomping around in the attic. "Fly away," I wanted to yell up into the attic one more time. There was silence, a few scraping sounds, and then he emerged with his instructions. "Just let it all stand as is for a month, then you can sweep it all into a paper bag and toss it into the garbage."

"Thank you for coming," I said as I walked him to the driveway. Just as he was about to pull away, he rolled down his window and said, "By the way, there were only a few bees in the hive. There could have been thousands. I don't know why there weren't more." He waved and then drove down the street.

A month later, I swept up fifty-four dead bees, scooped them into an old plastic soap tray, and buried the bees and the box in the backyard. I scraped the broken beehive into a paper bag and wished that I could reconstruct it and hang it in a tree.

Perhaps heaven is the reconstructed life hanging in another place.

Once, in the middle of a winter storm, I saw a sparrow suddenly appear on the fence post. This bird seemed undaunted by the wind and ice. It extended its wings and pushed off back into the storm.

That pleased me, and it made me think about what gives me the courage to push on. Faith in heaven's existence helps me overcome my fears and sustains me against the winter weather. I know such wind and ice—the death of my brother, the death of other people I have loved, the doubts about my writing. Much of my life came and went so quickly. It rustled like the leaves in the backyard trees. When I think about this, I feel sad, but then I realize how foolish I am to dare think that I have had a sad life, a lonely life, a life that did not bear much fruit. How could I think that when I look at Roe and our children and my students and my books?

The power of joy in my own life is what sustains me while the storm rages, while the snow beats down and the cold air fills my lungs. Like the sparrow, I extend my wings just the same and push off back into the storm. I take risks, I dare to love, I move forward even if the night is bleak. We human beings possess the courage and the faith to propel ourselves back into the storm and to discover the best part of living, the doing and the knowing.

The push into the winter night is all we need to know. No less, no more. When we know this, we can put things in perspective. We simply push off with our faith and our God. We fly away in victory and in joy.

THE BEST PART OF WINTER

I think I've seen the best part of winter,
The part I'll take when sadness leads to night
And I am an old man with little thought
Of what once held up against wind and ice.

It was a sudden visit and quick to leave.
The trees rattled against trees;
The sky was smeared with clouds and snow.
I looked out my window from where I was writing
And saw a sparrow atop the fence post.
It stopped, brushed up its feathers, turned its head.
All winter tried to knock it from the wooden peak,
But I know the power of what is weak
As the bird extended its wings
And pushed off into the bleak night:
No less, no more, just on its way still
Through the cold and constant storm.

This, the best part of winter.

My Friend Fred

In 1984, I lost my high school teaching job because of a drop in enrollment. I was the youngest member in the English department, so when the student population dropped, I was dropped. Roe was expecting a baby in July. My job would be over in June. I couldn't find another teaching position. We were facing a future without income or health insurance.

Then I was offered a job to work on a pilot for a children's television program. The man who offered me the job was Father John Catoir, the director, at the time, of the Christophers, an organization that celebrates goodness in the media and encourages people to strive for greatness no matter what they do with their lives. Its motto is "It's better to light one candle than to curse the darkness." The Christophers produces the television program *Christopher Closeup,* which features famous and not-so-famous people who all have one thing in common: they all made a significant difference in the world.

Father Catoir wanted the Christophers to develop a children's television program that would celebrate the idea that we can all make a difference in the world. He hired me to research children's television programs and to help develop the idea.

Shortly after I started, Father Catoir asked me to meet Fred Rogers, who was scheduled to be interviewed on *Christopher Closeup* at the HBO studio in New York. Fred was the creator and host of the famous children's TV program *Mister Rogers' Neighborhood.*

On the day of the interview, a program assistant took me to Fred's dressing room. She knocked on the door, warned me not to spend too much time there, and then opened the door and walked away. I poked my head into the room, and there, sitting on a folding chair, was the famous Fred Rogers, dressed in a blue sports jacket, a bow tie, beige pants, and loafers. As I sheepishly entered the room, he stood up from the chair and extended his hand in a warm greeting. "I am so pleased to meet you," he said. Nervously, I said I was also pleased to meet him, and then we both sat down.

Fred began our conversation by asking about me. He wanted to know about my teaching and about how I lost my job. I found myself telling him how frightened I had been when I lost my job, because Roe was about to have a baby. Fred asked me the name of our new daughter. Then he told me about his wife, Joanne, and their two boys. I took out pictures of Roe and the children from my wallet, and then Fred took out pictures of his family from his wallet, and we got along just fine.

We talked about books, music, loneliness, and memories. I barely mentioned the children's program I was trying to develop. Fred told me that I would be more than welcome to visit his studio in Pittsburgh if it would help my project.

We must have been talking for an hour when, suddenly, a team of studio people whisked Fred away for the *Christopher Closeup* taping. As he left, he shook my hand warmly and said, "Let's stay in touch."

I had to leave before the taping was over, so I didn't have a chance to say good-bye to Fred. I drove home that night feeling discouraged and embarrassed.

A few days later, the phone rang at our house. Roe answered it, spoke to the person on the other end for a few minutes, and then said to me, "Chris, it's Mister Rogers."

"Hello?" I said.

"Hello, Chris," Mr. Rogers said in his distinctive, genuine voice. "I didn't get a chance to say good-bye to you at the studio, and I wanted to thank you for telling me about your wife and children, and I wanted to thank you for showing me those wonderful pictures."

Then we started to talk again, picking up where we had left off. I told Fred that Karen, our new baby, was nearly walking. Fred spoke to me about Joanne and her professional piano career and how she was able to juggle this career with the responsibilities of being a wife and mother, and how proud of her he was. I told Fred that Roe worked for an orthodontist and was able to juggle her work with her responsibilities of being a wife and mother and that I was proud of her too. Then I spoke a little bit about my writing poetry, and he spoke a little about his writing music and the scripts for *Mister Rogers' Neighborhood*, and then he invited me to Pittsburgh again.

"Chris, I invited the poet May Sarton to the neighborhood. I think you would like her, seeing that you are also a poet. You could play a teacher coming to take May to a poetry reading at your school."

I was delighted. I accepted the invitation, and then I spoke about my poetry some more and about the struggles I have with trying to create beauty. As our conversation came to a close, Fred thanked me for giving *him* the time to talk with *me* on the phone. Then Fred said, "Bless your heart. You know who is in charge. Good-bye."

I did go to Pittsburgh. I met May Sarton, and we became close friends for the last ten years of her life. I was taped sitting on the swing with Mr. Rogers and May Sarton.

Two things happened to me that year because of Fred: I learned what friendship was all about, and I was able, for the first time in my life, to overtly speak about the existence of God in my writing.

When I met Fred, I had no friends. I had Roe and my parents and my brothers and sisters and my children, but because of my writing and teaching, I never had time for much of a social life.

That all changed once Fred and I started talking. For the past eighteen years, Fred and I have written letters to each other, visited each other's homes, e-mailed on a daily basis, and shared pictures and dinners. We have attended lectures together in New York, had dinner with Roe and Joanne, and shared the ups and downs of our regular routines. Once, I asked him why he extended himself to me, a goofy, nearly unemployed man who fiddled with poetry and didn't know very much about most things.

"Chris," Fred said, "when I first met you in that room at the HBO studio, you didn't want anything from me. You seemed interested in me, in my wife and children. You wanted to share those pictures of Roe and your children. I felt that you liked me, Fred, the person, not just Mister Rogers and his neighborhood."

In that first year of my friendship with Fred, I was sure that he would soon grow tired of me and return to more glamorous people. He would quickly discover that I was an ordinary man with a humble little house and bubbling dreams of being a writer, a man who led an ordinary life with a good wife and good children. But instead, I found out that Fred was an ordinary man with a humble home and bubbling dreams of being a writer and a musician, a man who led an ordinary life with a good wife and good children. He and I got along just fine. He liked me for me. I liked him for him.

The fact is that fame for people like Fred Rogers can easily cut you off from genuine relationships. Am I loved for me, or am I loved for what surrounds me? But my friendship with Fred was spared all that. I love Fred for who he is. He loves me for who I am, and all these years, he has nurtured me, given me advice and praise, and offered me wise, and sometimes tough, suggestions.

Fred taught me how to be a friend—how to be open and to be myself. Time and time again, he would end our phone conversations with the words "You know who is in charge." He helped me find the courage to speak about God, and then he let me say, aloud, how connected I feel to God when I write.

Fred has been one of the most significant forces in my spiritual life, because he helped me to say what I believe in my heart to be the truth about God's presence in the world, and in me. Writing poetry, singing, painting, sculpting, dancing . . . these are all evidence of God's presence within us.

Fred taught me not to be afraid to speak about my inner self. Fred helped me see that it is God's will that I write about grace. Fred taught me not to be afraid to say the name of God. When Fred speaks about writing music, he speaks with conviction about God's influence, God's will, and God's grace.

One of the central themes of Fred's television show is "I like you just the way you are." That all-embracing message is also God's message. It is, I believe, our responsibility to discover just who we are so that we can be fully ourselves in the glory of God's love for us.

A Prediction to Believe In

We are inundated with predictions these days. Political commentators predict the outcomes of elections before the final votes are tallied. Meteorologists predict snowstorms before even a single flake floats down from the mercurial sky. We rely on soothsayers and statisticians to determine the outcome of a football game and the behavior of the stock market. Some people in Japan claim that they can detect an illness before it strikes by scrutinizing the soles of people's feet. There are those who fear that the world will end in 2012, because that's when the Maya calendar runs out. People in India visit the town of Kanchipuram and pay to have their lives predicted by people who read palm leaves.

Sometimes it's entertaining to see whether or not predictions come true. When I was fifteen years old, our black cat, Moses, deposited a wiggling, pink, four-legged newborn creature on the back porch. No one knew what type of animal it was, but everyone had an idea. My brother said it was a kitten. My sister said it would grow up to be a pig. "It's a rat," I announced with confidence. My mother looked down with concern. "Well, whatever it is," she said, "it's hungry."

I quickly found a new eyedropper in the medicine cabinet, heated some milk on the stove, and tried feeding the mysterious animal. "Whatever it is," I said, "it sure can drink." We fed it day after day until, slowly, the hairless animal developed fur, wide eyes, and a long, full tail. A squirrel. Everyone's guess was wrong.

Many predictions about the future are based on similar guesswork. We look at something, see some future shape in our imaginations, and confidently make a prediction. Often this imagined future is simply an extension of the past. The stock market will go up next month because it's gone up for the last three. The Yankees will win the American League pennant because they've done so for the past three years. Our news agencies try to report stories before they happen.

It can be great fun when predictions fail. Schools in New Jersey were closed one recent winter day because meteorologists on television and on the radio predicted that we would experience one of the worst snowstorms in fifty years. They were wrong. Several inches of snow fell. I looked at my fifteen-year-old son as he entered the kitchen after sleeping until 8:30. "Why don't you call some of your friends and go sledding? At least there is enough snow for that."

Michael looked at me and said, "Hey, that's a good idea."

"I'll pick everybody up," I suggested, "and they can come back later for hot chocolate, and I'll treat everyone to pizza."

Michael logged on to AOL Instant Messenger and called friends on the phone at the same time. Within ten minutes, seven high school sophomores were all set to be picked up at 12:30. I predicted that they would have a great time. That prediction was correct.

The prediction of a catastrophic blizzard followed the pattern of many common prognostications. Something terrible is going to happen; evil will triumph as misfortune overtakes us. I think there's a difference between predictions based on what has happened in the past or on pessimistic outlooks and predictions based on faith, hope, and goodness. I think predictions of evil are often wrong. Surely they are wrong in an ultimate sense.

I am a person of faith. My mother predicted that my brother Oliver would be the first person to greet me in heaven, and I can hold on to that prediction and believe in it because I have faith.

I say, listen carefully—and skeptically—to what the news organizations are telling you. Listen to CNN, and then look at your children being good. Read *Newsweek,* and then watch your loved ones live each day with stamina and courage. Don't believe that news programs and newspapers always project what is really happening in the world, or what might happen. Do not be misled by their dire predictions. Understand that the media experts are trying to grab our attention. A fifteen year old who shoots thirteen people in a high school is terrible news. Goodness, like a rich autumn crop, is not news at all.

I liked watching that hairless animal develop into a fat, gray squirrel. I liked listening to my son's teenage friends singing together over pizza and soda. I like thinking about dancing with my brother in heaven.

Should I listen to Dan Rather's view of the world or my mother's? That's an easy choice.

American Laughter

Some people believe we have lost the American laughter. A student at the high school where I teach said, "If Huckleberry Finn was around today, he wouldn't lean back on his raft and chuckle and dream about catching pirates." This is true enough. Today, we're more likely to complain about the sad look on the Statue of Liberty or about the sorry news oozing out from Washington, D.C., and Wall Street than laugh.

But in my opinion, America seems to be all about laughter—even today. If it isn't, what then is the purpose of fireworks and hotdogs, sleigh rides down Sam's Hill, the Sadie Hawkins dance over at the high school tonight, and the scent of honeysuckle? It seems to me that these things are all about laughter.

Some people want to reclaim the past. We want Norman Rockwell painting Main Street scenes and boys running down to Cutter's Pond. We miss the times when the Cracker Jack boxes really did have neat prizes.

We can't return to the past. But the laughter hasn't left the present.

Some recent events at the school where I teach might help prove my point. I work in the second largest high school in New Jersey. The school population includes children from Lebanon, Puerto Rico, India, Poland, Hungary, Colombia, and China and third-generation children from Italy, France, Ireland, and Germany. We have children from Peru and Pakistan, Romania and Russia. People say that things are not what they once were. America today isn't like the America of the past. Kids are shooting kids. Teenagers have no respect; they use vulgar language, drink, have lots of sex, are lazy, watch too much television, lack ambition, and just don't seem to laugh much anymore. I'd like to put these ideas to the test.

I was sitting in my office when Brian rushed into the room, pulled a chair up to my desk, flopped down, and said, "Dr. de Vinck, you've got to help me with my college essay. My dad says that if I don't finish it, I can't go out tonight with my girlfriend." I laughed and laughed, and Brian began to laugh, and then we settled down to review his essay.

Kathy told me this morning that she broke up with her boyfriend of six months. "Six months is a long time," I said with a long, serious smile. She smiled too, and then she started to giggle.

On Monday, Yassmin stopped me in the hall and nearly whispered, "Dr. de Vinck. Do you have any books to read? I like romance novels." Then she blushed and laughed. I gave her Betty Smith's *Joy in the Morning,* which she finished in two days. This afternoon I gave her *Dr. Zhivago.*

Last week one of our Muslim students greeted me with a beautiful smile. Her smiling face was wrapped in her beige veil. She was as beautiful as a black-eyed Susan. I said good morning and asked how her day was going. "It is well. I have made a decision. I will enter the Muslim school next year so that I can learn to be a teacher of my faith." I congratulated her and said that such a decision is filled with a mysterious good. She laughed and understood probably better than I ever will.

Today in school, I observed six classes. In one, I saw students wearing crowns of laurel leaves stand before their class and read from *Julius Caesar.* In another class, the students were singing aloud the ballads they had written the night before for their British-literature class. Every student gave out a laugh of delight after finishing his or her presentation.

In one class I looked in on, the students were silently reading *To Kill a Mockingbird,* and the teacher whispered, "Boo Radley is watching over all of us with goodness and laughter." Down the hall, a freshman class was hooting with glee at a part from a book by P. G. Wodehouse that their teacher was reading aloud.

In the hall this morning, I found myself walking a few steps behind two girls who were laughing and laughing. I said, in my best administrator's voice, "Girls. You know there is no laughing in the halls." They turned to me with a hesitant air of serious silence, and then they laughed even louder. "Hi, Dr. de Vinck," they said, and then they laughed some more.

Last night I went to the spring concert and watched the teenagers play their trumpets, flutes, and violins with grace and passion. I listened to the choir sing hymns of praise that would shatter the heart of the most stoic monk.

We are not a sad nation. We are not a nation of guns and shooting and lost dreams. The stock market does not define us or our nation. We are too easily duped into sadness by our news organizations.

America is not a single idea or an exclusive group of people. America is a British-literature class with kids whose parents believe in God, Buddha, Allah, Abraham. We might not have great surprises inside the Cracker Jack boxes any longer, but we have, more than ever, a continent filled with a people that are better educated, better fed, and better housed than at any other time in the history of the world. We are a nation where opportunity is available to the immigrant's son and to the president's daughter.

Brian finished his college essay and was allowed to go out with his girlfriend that night. Kathy is already dating her old boyfriend's brother. I know Yassmin will fall in love with Dr. Zhivago and that some day, my smiling Muslim student is going to be a happy Muslim teacher smiling over the heads of her students.

If Norman Rockwell were alive today, he would have no problem finding the right images for his easel. I say bah humbug to all the pessimists dismissing our ability to laugh. I say shame on you to all who believe that money and politics are the engines that drive our American spirit.

The laughter of Huckleberry Finn is far more in our blood than are the numbers of the stock exchange.

Wild Man

Sometimes I wish I could roll around on the ground of the African veldt under the hot sun of a tropical sky, shake my hair, and taste the raw flesh torn from the flanks of a zebra, as I have seen lions do on nature programs. But this is a fantasy. I am not a lion. I have been tamed. It is the taming of the beast inside of us that allows us to be human.

Such calm is the infusion of the Holy Spirit. Somewhere along the line, we evolved from wild creatures into people who have the potential to pray, to love, and to build a portal to heaven. Yet every day, we struggle with the two parts of our nature: the savage and the civilized, the pagan and the saintly.

As we build our own small paradise here on earth, we grow closer to heaven's gate. My paradise, my Eden, my heaven on earth is home with Roe and our children. I want to teach my son Michael that he doesn't have to travel to Australia in search of heaven's existence. Heaven can be found right in his own backyard. All Michael has to do is repeat the words Dorothy chanted as she clicked her ruby shoes together at the end of *The Wizard of Oz*: "There's no place like home."

Having traveled all over the world, I have come to realize that my backyard is as close to Eden as I will ever get on this earth. Make no mistake—wildness flourishes in my little Eden. In the twenty-four years that I have lived in this house, I have come across many different creatures in the little garden of grass and pachysandra: skunks digging in the dirt in search of grubs, a raccoon staring at me from a low tree branch with an empty tuna-fish can in its paws. I have found the prints of deer in the snow, a rabbit hole, ladybugs, fireflies.

This afternoon I raked the leaves in my little backyard, the yard that is filled with oak trees and confined by a green wire fence. As I raked, the dog chased the leaves that flew up in the air. It was cold outside. My neighbor offered me a leaf blower, but I declined, giving the excuse that I needed the exercise. I didn't tell him that while I raked, I imagined setting a trap for a polar bear or making a pile of leaves as tall as a haystack with my own labor. If you look out your window and see your neighbor raking his lawn, you see gloves, a hat, green pants, and work shoes, the shape of an ordinary man, the rake in hand. It must be a man, you think. But don't be so sure. Could it be a hunter with a spear and wild hair?

Last summer I spent a few weeks in Belgium with my cousins. I had time to visit family and time to sleep, time to read and time to walk along the edge of fields that had once been the battlegrounds of Waterloo, world wars, and the Visigoths. Fields of wheat stretched beyond my vision. Red poppies grew at my feet along the edge of the field.

As I continued on my way, I came upon a farmhouse, an inner court and stables, and a large field, where a single white horse galloped. A man in the field chased after the horse, waving his hat and swearing angrily in French. The horse ran to the edge of the field, and then, in a steady leap, it rose up and flew over the wooden fence. I could see the muscles of its legs and back working together to carry it over the fence and bring it down onto the ground on the other side. The horse then ran off through an open field of green and sky and distant trees. The farmer threw his hat on the ground and swore some more.

I thought about the wild horse as I finished raking the lawn. The sun had set and the moon was rising in the east. My arms ached. My legs were tense. I leaned my rake against a tree, sat on the cold ground, and looked up at the moon making her way, once again, along her usual route. I pulled my legs up to my chest and felt like the boy in the famous Andrew Wyeth painting, the boy sitting in the field wearing a raccoon-skin hat. Then, without provocation, I stood up and began to run toward the fence. I, the wild horse, the panting boy, ran to the fence and then jumped over it, landing in a large pile of leaves. Perhaps I roared like a lion or neighed like a horse. I felt like a man who had escaped for a moment. I had fled the eye of the moon, the embrace of the responsible fence that holds in the oak trees and the grass and the small space that I pretend to control, my paradise.

I stood up, opened the gate, and stepped back into the yard. I placed the rake in the shed and called for the dog. Just before I entered the house, I brushed a leaf from my sleeve and watched it spin to the ground. I ran my hand through my hair, walked in, and then closed the door, the portal to heaven: my home, my backyard, my wife and children.

As the wild and tame sides of our nature battle, we seek the still place of peace within. After all the fuss we make in our daily living, after all the traveling and visiting, after all the things we have seen in museums and have read about in books, in the end we long for a single image, a single essence. We can peel away all of our earthly desires and possessions one at a time until the center is revealed, something mundane but beautiful—a gray barrel brimming with rainwater, God in heaven—a center that we can know and possess. We all seek the center—the central image that compresses everything we know into one poem or idea or prayer.

For me, after all my longing and traveling and seeking, I have found my center. It is my home, my backyard, my heaven on earth.

STILL LIFE

Perhaps, after all, it is just a gray barrel
Against the white shed under the drain spout,

Not self, not a lost sparrow in the yard
Perched on a branch of the mock-orange bush,
Shaking its feathers.

I once thought it was the sun on my floor
As I turned my hand in the honey light.

I searched in my books of poetry,
Found Byzantium and mermaids singing
Each to each, and spring pools and sweet plums.

I traveled to the museums, admired
Gerard's Psyche and L'Amour,
Applauded the dancers of Degas,
Admired the blue colors of Vermeer.

I saw Paris and Rome, the grandfather clock of London,
Windmills of Holland with outstretched arms.

I felt the urge to proclaim it was Niagara Falls
Or the Grand Canyon, the Painted Desert or Mt. Shasta.

But in my wide search, I found all along that
It is there just so, sitting in the backyard:

My gray barrel filled with rainwater.

Tap Me on the Shoulder

I was driving to the store to buy a newspaper, and Michael had come along for the ride. As we drove along, I turned to Michael and said, "You know what, Michael?"

"I know," he said with feigned exasperation. "You love me."

"Now how did you know I was going to say that?" I asked with feigned puzzlement.

"You always tell me that," he said. Then he looked over at me. "You forgot to put your seat belt on."

I reached back for the seat belt and pulled it across my waist, locking it into place. We continued on our way.

When I think about this moment, I am reminded of the time my flight from Newark to Detroit was cancelled and I had to fly into Cleveland to catch a connecting flight to Detroit.

When our plane arrived in Cleveland, those of us flying on to Detroit were put on a bus. The driver drove us around the terminal, past a 747, past another large jet craft, and past the control tower. We drove through the darkness and out beyond the airport, where we stopped. In front of us was an airplane, or at least it *looked* like an airplane. It was a small machine with two propellers. I and the rest of the passengers walked up a narrow flight of stairs into the plane.

There were nine seats on the left and nine seats on the right. We sat down and buckled our seat belts as a man in a white shirt stepped out from the cockpit. He smiled. "I'll come around and check your seat belts. We will be leaving shortly." Then he checked each of our seat belts and made sure we were strapped in securely.

"I'll be your captain for tonight's flight," he said as he returned to the front of the plane and reached for a rope. He gave the rope a quick tug, and the door shut with a thud.

"Now let me show you how to open this door in case there is an emergency. Just pull this latch," he said, struggling with the latch, "and at the same time push this white button." He pushed the white button and wiggled the latch some more. "Now let's hope that if we have an emergency, you won't have as much difficulty as I am having." He smiled when the door finally opened. "To close the door, just pull on the rope and push the latch down like this." We heard a precise click. "Right."

The captain stood up and began to walk into the cockpit. Then he turned and said, "During the flight, if anyone is cold, just come up and tap me on the shoulder, and I'll turn up the heat."

It's good to have people looking out for you on your travels.

When we got to the newspaper store, Michael reminded me that he liked Slim Jims.

"Michael, I only brought sixty cents for the newspaper," I said, digging into my coat pocket as if to show him I had no more money.

He looked at me and then put his sock-covered feet on the hot-air vent on the dashboard. I closed the car door and walked into the store.

"Hello, Charles," I said to the store manager.

"Hello, Chris."

"Do you have any Slim Jims?"

"Yes, on the shelf where the candy is."

I found the small pot and looked for the price of the Slim Jim stick: eighty-nine cents. Once again I fished around in my coat pocket, and this time I found a dollar bill. I picked up a newspaper and paid for it and the salami stick.

On our way home, I pulled out the Slim Jim and gently bonked Michael on the head with it. He took it in silence.

As I turned onto our street, Michael said, "You know what, Dad?"

"Yeah. I know. You love me," I said in feigned exasperation. I pulled into the driveway and shut off the car.

"How'd you know?" he asked with pretend puzzlement. Then he jumped out of the car and ran into the house, saying over his shoulder, "It's freezing out here!"

"That's because you don't have on your coat! And you're running in your stocking feet!" I yelled after him, smiling. He was already in the house. I looked up and saw that the moon was climbing out of the trees and on its way to heaven.

Someday Michael will know that if he ever gets cold, he can tap me on the shoulder, and I will turn up the heat.

Someday Michael will know that I am the old man dying in Australia and that this book is my message and promise to him that heaven does exist.

CONTACT THE AUTHOR

Christopher de Vinck has been invited to speak at universities, churches, hospitals, national conventions, and the Vatican. He delivers speeches on family, faith, disabilities, education, fatherhood, and writing. He can be contacted at devinck@sprynet.com or at 11 Woodland Court, Pompton Plains, NJ 07444.